D1627473

NORFOLK LIBRARY
AND INFORMATION SERVICE

# STRIKE HARD

## A BOMBER AIRFIELD AT WAR

# STRIKE HARD

## A BOMBER AIRFIELD AT WAR

RAF Downham Market and its Squadrons
1942–46

JOHN B. HILLING

ALAN SUTTON PUBLISHING LIMITED

First published in the United Kingdom in 1995
Alan Sutton Publishing Limited · Phoenix Mill · Far Thrupp · Stroud · Gloucestershire

British Library Cataloguing in Publication Data

A catalogue record for this book is available from the British Library.

ISBN 0–7509–0969–2

Typeset in 10/12pt Times.
Typesetting and origination by
Alan Sutton Publishing Ltd.
Printed in Great Britain by
Butler & Tanner, Frome, Somerset.

This book is dedicated to all the young men who flew from Downham Market and who, in good faith, gave their lives that we who remained might prosper.

# Contents

# List of Illustrations

# MAPS

# Foreword

GROUP CAPTAIN T.G. 'HAMISH' MAHADDIE DSO, DFC, AFC, CZMC, CENG, FRAES

*Hamish Mahaddie flew two tours of operations with RAF Bomber Command during the Second World War before joining Air Vice-Marshal Don Bennett's Staff at HQ 8 (Pathfinder) Group. He finished the war as station commander at RAF Warboys, home of the PFF Navigation Training Unit.*

Although Downham Market was possibly the last station to be appended to 8 (PFF) Group, Air Vice-Marshal Don Bennett, the AOC, decreed that it must have an equal amount of attention from the Group's staff and certainly an even fuller share of visits, in spite of Downham being the furthest in distance from the Group Headquarters at Huntingdon. In any event Downham had more than its fair share of Pathfinder Force (PFF) characters serving there as pathfinders.

The main squadron at Downham was No. 635, formed in March 1944 from one of the founder PFF squadrons, No. 35. It retained much of the glamour and the high operational experience of the mother squadron, but soon built a reputation in its own right on operations.

Most conspicuous perhaps among Downham's PFF characters was Alex Thorne, whose sortie tally is obscure but certainly no fewer than eighty by the time he finished his third tour.

Another larger than life original pathfinder was Tubby Baker, who commanded 635 Squadron. A superb pathfinder and an outstanding master bomber, he was perhaps one of the best known of our squadron commanders, who looked very likely to complete his third tour.

One-time Air Staff Officer at PFF HQ, Arty Ashworth was a famous pilot with 635 Squadron. Also ex-35 and 156 Squadrons, he was one of the founder members of the original PFF. Arty was one of a select few captains who, upon finding his aircraft on fire due to heavy flak over the target area, ordered the entire crew to bail out. As the fire appeared to intensify, and he was very near the highest part of the Alps, he put the aircraft into a dive and found to his surprise the slipstream put the flames out. Then, without a crew, he managed to navigate to the French coast and hence to the UK, and by following the identification letters being flashed in Morse on RAF airfields he found his way back to base. Oddly enough the CO of 35 Squadron, Wing Commander Robinson, did exactly the same thing very shortly afterwards and was awarded a Bar to his DSO for his effort. Ashworth only remembers a right royal rocket he received from Don Bennett and he was never able to understand what the difference was between his solo effort and that of Wing Commander Robinson.

One more outstanding character on 635 Squadron was 'Pluto' Cousens, a navigator whom I personally recommended to command a PFF squadron. Sadly he was lost very early in his tour – and possibly on his first flight as a squadron commander: a serious loss to the station and the pathfinders.

Downham was graced by two holders of the Victoria Cross, both of whom received the award posthumously. Flight Sergeant Aaron of 218 Squadron was a most promising junior candidate for the pathfinders and for high rank. Nevertheless his citation gives some clue as to his regard for duty and the degree of his ability to carry out pathfinder tactics. The second holder of the Victoria Cross was Squadron Leader Bazalgette of 635 Squadron, originally from Calgary,

Canada, who was brought to the UK by his parents in early childhood. During a daylight raid, while acting as Master Bomber, his Lancaster was attacked, severely damaged and set on fire. He ordered the crew to bail out and then attempted to land the aircraft, which, sadly, broke up on impact and he perished in the crash with the other crew.

Like most pathfinder stations Downham seemed to have a large hardcore of outstanding NCO aircrew and I am reminded of one, a rear gunner named Douglas Cameron. A gillie from north of the border, Cameron actually bailed out of two PFF aircraft, both of whose captains were subsequently awarded Victoria Crosses. Douglas Cameron not only bailed out of Bazalgette's aircraft but also was ordered out of Edwin Swale's. Cameron managed to evade capture by using his field craft to ford rivers and streams, to break his scent and climb trees to evade searching Germans with dog patrols. A remarkable double for an NCO gunner, whose death was only recently announced when he was well into his eighties.

Some more fine Downham PFF types are Jimmy Dow, another 'ton-up' specialist; Denis Whit, a Halton 'brat' and further a colleague; and Reggie Cox, the station commander and also a Halton 'brat', all of whom enriched Downham with their operational flair and personality. Reggie Cox was the first of my fellow 'brats' from the leafy hills surrounding Halton, Bucks, and he was followed by many more whom I recruited and trained with a view to becoming flight and squadron commanders, although several did in fact command PFF stations in the group to great effect. The fabric of the entire force was strengthened by these outstanding and highly experienced pathfinders who lived – and some died – during the years of Harris's bomber offensive in the Second World War.

Downham Market suffered approximately the same losses inflicted on other pathfinder stations and 635 Squadron was certainly in the van on the night of the Nuremberg raid on 30/31 March 1944 – a disaster which should never have happened. Normally 8 Group and Don Bennett planned the routing for Command on each sortie. On this occasion the PFF route was debated at Bomber Command on a tele link-up between headquarters and the group commanders. In view of the latest Pampa (Mossie Met Report) relayed by a Met Flight aircraft on sight over the route, Bennett and the AOC of 4 Group, Roddy Carr, made a plea on the link-up that the long single leg from Cologne to near Nuremberg should be abandoned. A considerable disagreement between the parties involved resulted in the decision, by a single vote, that the sortie to Nuremberg should be mounted in spite of the changed weather forecast, and to include the long leg. The result was that some ninety-three aircraft were lost on the Nuremberg sortie, the worst defeat suffered by the Command during the entire bomber offensive.

There appears to be no report or record of this tele link-up and we only have an account of what happened, by word of mouth, from Don Bennett. I personally have been told by Willi Herget, a well-known Luftwaffe nightfighter pilot with some eighty-five official kills to his credit, that it was impossible not to guess where the final target was to be because of the line of burning British aircraft on the ground, which stretched unbroken from near Cologne to the turning point for Nuremberg.

Downham was a FIDO station and although this attracted occasional Luftwaffe intruders there is no record of any Downham aircraft ever being destroyed by the Luftwaffe over Downham itself. We have, however, a brief account by Leutnant Heinz Wolfgang Schnaufer, a leading Luftwaffe nightfighter ace with some 121 kills to his credit, that he was unable to effect any losses on Downham aircraft while visiting the FIDO-equipped station. Willi Herget was also unsuccessful visiting Downham while the FIDO was burning.

Over Germany the Mossie pilots of 608 Squadron were frequently attacked by the new Luftwaffe jet, the Me262, but as far as we were able to discover they were brief attacks without any kills.

Thus, in the closing moments of the war, after the last bombs had been hoisted into a Lanc or Mosquito and dropped on Germany, the warm heart of Downham Market was suddenly still. With the end of the war in Europe now a reality after six years of fighting, the RAF and the good burghers of Downham Market joined together and celebrated victory with many parties in Downham and district. Many a night there was dancing in the market square of the town and inevitably someone was to hoist a pair of WAAF 'blackouts' (knickers), on the mayor's flagpole. And finally someone had to reach the town clock to stop the hands at 2230 hours – the official timing of the end of hostilities in Europe. The person responsible was easily identifiable: he was, of course, an Ozzie wearing the navy blue uniform of the RAAF – 'good on you, cobber.'

Once the celebrations had subsided the sound and the fury of Downham Market was silent. Aircraft and crews were spirited away; the superb groundcrews were re-assigned throughout the air force, some going to Tiger Force in the Far East; a few were demobbed, making their individual ways back to Wagga Wagga in the Oz, to the sheep and hot springs of New Zealand, or the snowy wastes of a grim winter in Canada; or indeed nearer home to some croft in the Highlands, or to Wigan in the north-west of England.

The townspeople dearly missed the personnel at Downham, who had become part and parcel of a large local family. In a few short months the airfield had reverted to its original role as a satellite of RAF Marham. The landing ground itself was given back to the local owners from whom it had been requisitioned in the war, buildings were demolished or taken over by the local council, the runways were broken up and the concrete used as hardcore for local new roads. The entire locale returned to a grateful peace and today the only memory left at RAF Downham Market is a simple plaque in the church of St Mary's, Bexwell.

And yet the memories of these difficult and exciting times have not faded from the minds of those who did strive and suffer as aircrew at Downham. For instance, Alex Thorne decreed in his Will that, when he died, those of his crew who survived him should identify the dispersal pan on the airfield perimeter where their Lanc rested between sorties, and scatter his ashes there. This was duly carried out by Boris Bressloff, his H2S set operator, and Harry Parker, his flight engineer, after Alex died in 1990.

*T G Mahaddie*

Group Captain T.G. Mahaddie RAF (Retd)
January 1995

# Acknowledgements

A book of this nature inevitably owes a very large debt to other people and organizations. In particular, many people have delved into the past and drawn on their memories to furnish me with information which I could not possibly have otherwise discovered. Others have generously helped me by making available their own photographs and other material. My main source of information came from searching through the Royal Air Force records in the Public Record Office. This material would, however, have been mere dry facts without the knowledge and anecdotes passed on to me by airmen and airwomen who served at RAF Downham Market between 1942 and 1946 and who actually witnessed the events described in this book. They are listed below according to their squadrons, etc. My sincerest thanks to them all.

**218 Squadron, 1942–44**
Corporal Eric Basford.
Flight Lieutenant Roy B. Belderson, AFC.
Flight Lieutenant Maxie Booth.
Pilot Officer Reg Davey.
Leading Aircraftsman Wyndham Dickenson.
Sergeant Len W.J. Durrant.
Leading Aircraftsman Sydney M. Jones.
Group Captain O.A. Morris.
Leading Aircraftsman Bill J.A. Overton.
Corporal W. Pinnigar.
Sergeant Ian A. Robb.
Squadron Leader Geoff M. Rothwell.
Squadron Leader Ian Ryall.
Sergeant Lyndon O. Sims, DFC.
Squadron Leader Laurence E. Skan.
Sergeant Charles F. Weir.

**608 Squadron, 1944–45**
Flight Lieutenant Harry S.T. Harris, DFC.
Flight Lieutenant P.S. Hobbs, DFC.
Flight Lieutenant Cecil R. Jacobs, DFC.
Flight Lieutenant Charles Lockyer.
Squadron Leader Peter A.C. McDermott, DFC, DFM.
Flight Lieutenant George A. Nunn, DFC.
Squadron Leader V.G. Robson, DFC and Bar.
Flying Officer B.J. Sherry, DFC.

**623 Squadron, 1943**
Leading Aircraftsman F. Len Warner.

**635 Squadron, 1944–45**
Flight Sergeant Johnny P.G. Baines.
Wing Commander S. 'Tubby' Baker, DSO, DFC.
Sergeant Basil Brown.
Flying Officer Jack Catford, DFC.
Flight Sergeant Paddy Cronin.
Sergeant J. Donald Eastwood.
Flying Officer Charles Godfrey.
Flight Sergeant Alan C. Hartley.
Flight Sergeant Wally H. Hitchcock, DFM.
Sergeant Patrick Nolan.
Flight Sergeant William D. Ogilvie.
Flight Lieutenant G. Alex Thorne, DSO, DFC.
Flight Lieutenant Ronald H. Wright, DFC, DFM.

**Women's Auxiliary Air Force, 1943–45**
Mrs Peggy Moorcroft (nee Sergeant 'Tommy' Thompson).
Mrs Eleanor M. Zaleski (nee Corporal Bignall).

**Other RAF Ground Staff, 1942–45**
Leading Aircraftsman Herbert F. Crisp.
Corporal H.W.S. Gable.
Leading Aircraftsman G.K. Green.
Flying Officer W.F. Provis.
Corporal Jack Tukelove.

I would also like to thank the following individuals for their valuable help: Ron Bennett; Sergeant Don Bruce (115 Squadron); M.S. Bullen; F. Ron Chapell; G. Clout, Imperial War Museum; Paul Dascombe; Jonathan Falconer; Dennis H. Foreman; Bob Fuller; David A.L. Hilling; Mrs Joan A.F. Horton; Mr and Mrs Reg Kent; J.D. Llewellin, French Kier Construction; Group Captain Hamish Mahaddie for his foreword; J. Monk, Editor, *Air Mail*; John Reid; Bruce Robertson; Steve C. Smith; A. Williams, Imperial War Museum; G. Williams.

Grateful acknowledgement is also made here for the use of copyright material as follows: to Jonathan Falconer and Ian Allan Ltd, for an extract from *Stirling at War*; to 'Archie' Hall and Merlin Books Ltd, for extracts from *We, Also, Were There*; to Bill Jackson and Turner-Warwick Publications Inc, for an extract from *Three Stripes and Four Brownings*; to Laddie Lucas and Hutchinson Ltd, for an extract from *Out of the Blue*; to Alexander McKee and Souvenir Press for extracts from *The Mosquito Log*; to Malcolm Metchem for a quotation from the *Eastern Daily Press*; to Martin Middlebrook for extracts from *The Battle of Hamburg – The Firestorm Raid* and *The Nuremberg Raid, 30–31 March 1944*, reproduced by permission of Penguin Books Ltd; to Murray Peden and Canada's Wings Inc, for an extract from *A Thousand Shall Fall*; to David J. Smith and Patrick Stephens Ltd, an imprint of Haynes Publishing, for an extract from *Britain's Military Airfields 1939–45*; to The Salamander Oasis Trust and Dent/Everyman's Library for the poem 'We, The Bombers', by P. Heath, printed in *Poems of the Second World War: The Oasis Selection*, 1985; to The Stirling Aircraft Association for quotations from its *Journal* and *Newsletter*; and to Alex Thorne and Ian Allan Ltd, for an extract from *Lancaster at War 4*.

# Introduction

This is the story of one small cog in the machinery of the Second World War – the story of an airfield in East Anglia where every night for three long years young men flew off to wage battle against the enemy across the English Channel. But, like any cog in a well-designed piece of machinery, it was a vital component of British military strategy and without it and many others like it who knows how much longer the war might have lasted. The airfield at Bexwell, near Downham Market, was unusual in a number of ways and has its own unique history stemming both from the men and women who served on it and from the events which took place there during that stirring period. In many other ways, however, the airfield was typical of hundreds of other airfields that were hastily constructed all over eastern England during the early years of the war when the threat from Nazi Germany was at its highest. The history of RAF Downham Market is thus not only a record of a particular airfield but also the story in microcosm of Bomber Command during the war years.

My earliest recollection of the airfield is a hazy one; distantly I remember it being constructed. I was seven years old then and must have first seen the airfield, or the aerodrome as we called it, during a Sunday walk with my parents and my sister. Soon the aerodrome and the planes that flew from it were to be the ever-present background of my boyhood, so much so, indeed, that it seemed that they had always been part of my life. At night I went to sleep to the sounds of aircraft taking off on their way to Germany; in the day-time the sky seemed to be never without some aircraft in it, while even the classroom of our little village school was hung with models of different aircraft. And so it was with many an East Anglian boy and girl; our lives were filled with the sounds of aircraft and with stories of the airmen and airwomen living on and flying from the aerodromes interspersed amongst the fields between our villages and towns.

But boyhood memories are not enough; nor are they reliable. I wanted to know more about what had happened on my doorstep. In order to find out how and why and what had happened I had to search through old books and newspapers and long-forgotten files and ask many questions. And so this book was born.

In writing this book I have tried to show all aspects of life and work on and off the airfield. In order to do this and, at the same time, give some meaning to the organization of a war-time bomber station and the way in which bombing operations were conducted each chapter is devoted to a particular activity or situation. I have deliberately avoided making a chronological record of all operations, but have concentrated on highlights in the air and on minor details on the ground to re-create, as far as possible, the atmosphere of those days. To help in that re-creation I have quoted liberally from letters and interviews of those who served at Downham Market. I make no apology for using other people's words: they, after all, were there; I was not.

Except in that which comes through in the quotations mentioned above I have not tried to describe the real horrors of war-time operations. For one who did not experience at first-hand the events in the air a truthful description would be impossible. The reader must imagine the stink of oil in the fuselage, the incessant noise of the engines, the piercing, freezing cold of flying in uninsulated aircraft, the long hours cramped in a gun turret, the searing brightness of searchlights, the cries of excitement and pain, the blood and dismembered limbs of wounded colleagues, the sweat, vomit and excrement of fear. Fear was not confined to a few. The reality of flying night after night over enemy territory made fear ever present, for eventually nearly all aircrew would have been, had they continued long enough, either killed or maimed for life, or suffered mental breakdowns.

We may never know how successful the campaign of Bomber Command was; or whether or not it weakened Germany materially more than it helped strengthen the German resolve. What we do know is that the cost, both to the allied airmen and to the German people, was enormous. Downham Market played a vital part in Bomber Command's campaign; but it also paid a heavy price. Nearly a thousand young men gave their lives and many more were gravely injured. Their memorial is in St Mary's church, Bexwell. Their graves lie, for the most part, scattered in foreign fields.

John B. Hilling

## CHAPTER I

# Hesitant Beginnings

A bout a mile east of Downham Market the road to Swaffham passes close to a small Norman church partially hidden by a nineteenth-century rectory, a hall and some farm buildings, and a fifteenth-century gatehouse. This is Bexwell and the church, with its distinctive round tower is St Mary's church. On the lawn at the side of the lane leading to the church there is a bronze plaque on which are recorded the names of two very courageous men who each posthumously won the Victoria Cross. They, twenty year old Squadron Leader Ian Bazalgette and twenty-one year old Flight Sergeant Arthur Aaron, were pilots of Bomber Command during the Second World War and were stationed on the airfield which once stood on the opposite side of the road. More than eight hundred other young aircrew also lost their lives in the service of their country whilst flying on bombing missions from the airfield between 1942 and 1945. Many more airmen were badly wounded or became prisoners of war.

On the chancel wall of St Mary's church there is a plaque commemorating the men of the five squadrons which regularly flew from the Bexwell aerodrome, or RAF Downham Market as it was officially designated. The airfield has disappeared from sight now and the church is hardly used. Ironically, the church was frequented more during war-time than during the peace which followed. Aircrew often visited the church and one aircraftsman had the duty of looking

*St Mary's church, Bexwell.*

after the stove to heat the church. Often aircrew used to call in to pray before going out on operations. Sometimes they left an odd coin there for the padre. One airman, who used to call in on his way back after a night on duty, affirmed that: 'I never went to church at home, but I like to come in here.' Another returning airman called it 'a peaceful oasis in a mad world'.[1]

If one looks across the fields surrounding the church and takes in the quiet scene it is difficult not to believe that it was always so. The fields are unusually large and are intensively cultivated. There are very few hedgerows, but in the distance small clumps of trees can be seen. Rarely do visitors come to disturb the agricultural peace. It seems timeless and unchanging. Nevertheless, for four years during the Second World War, the scene was one of ceaseless activity in every direction both on the ground and in the air. Now, however, there is virtually nothing to see of what was the airfield or to suggest all that frenetic energy. The concrete runways have all been taken up and the myriad buildings have mostly come down. Cereal crops grow where dozens of aircraft once stood waiting and trees and scrub have colonized again the places where thousands of men and women from all over Britain and all parts of the Commonwealth once lived.

Four years may seem a brief and insignificant part of a lifetime but these particular years were probably the most memorable period in the lives both of those people stationed on the airfield and of those people who lived in the nearby towns and villages. Like it or not, it was impossible not to be acutely aware of the aerial activity overhead and of the cruel war being fought almost from the doorsteps of the houses and farms. Every day the vast sky was enlivened by innumerable aircraft on training and practice flights. Every night the stillness of the air was rudely broken by the raucous sound of aircraft setting out on their deadly missions.

When the time came to return to base in the early hours of the morning often one or two, and on occasions three, aircraft were missing and failed to arrive – the much hoped-for return of their young crews having been permanently delayed by death. Even when crews were able to bring their aircraft back the planes were often so badly damaged, or so short of fuel, that they crashed in nearby fields or on the airfield itself as they were coming in to land. Then there were the accidents to aircraft taking off, accidental bomb explosions, enemy intruder raids, occasional sounds of gunfire, the criss-crossing of searchlights probing the night sky and, later on in the war, the strange fiery glow of the fog dispersal system in winter.

Although, at the time, they could have had little idea of what was to be in store for them few people locally welcomed the prospect of a Bomber Command airfield in their midst. Apart from the obvious problems associated with aircraft noise, increased road traffic and the possibility of reprisal raids the base also meant dispossession, eviction, destruction, loss of fox-hunting land, closure of roads and a general disruption of the rural way of life, to say nothing of the disturbance to traditional standards and values which war inevitably always brings.

The airfield, or aerodrome as it was known, was brought into being as a result of an expansion programme conceived after the Second World War had started. Soon after the outbreak of war it became urgently necessary to build many more airfields for the Royal Air Force's Bomber Command – and later, still more for the United States' Army Air Force – in order to take the battle back to Nazi-controlled Germany. Norfolk, being one of the parts of Britain nearest to Germany, inevitably took the brunt of this rapid development of aviation bases. In September 1939, at the start of the war, there had been only four fully operational military airfields in the county: at Marham, Feltwell, Watton and West Raynham. By the end of hostilities in 1945 the number of military airfields in Norfolk had risen to thirty-seven of which no less than thirty-one were used by Bomber Command.

Marham, eight miles north-east of Downham Market, had been re-opened in 1937 as a two-squadron bomber airfield. It now came within 3 Group of Bomber Command and had its own

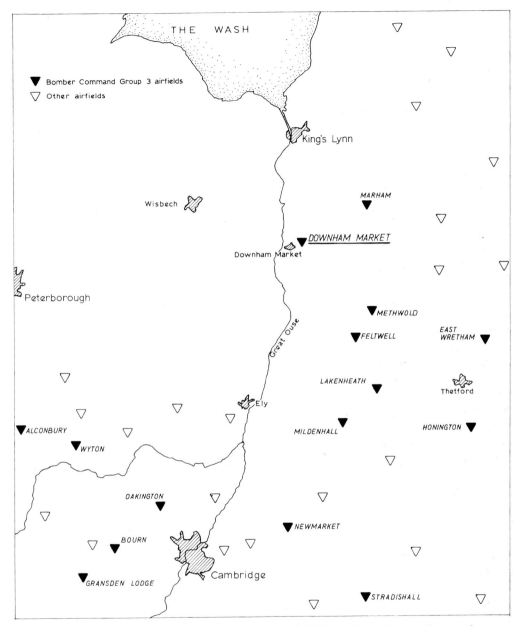

*The location of RAF Downham Market in relation to other airfields in 3 Group Bomber Command, as at July 1942.*

satellite landing ground at Barton Bendish. The Barton Bendish landing ground was rudimentary in the extreme; being little more than a very large grass field with a few tents and a bren-gun turret. Nonetheless, two-engined Wellington bombers were dispersed there from time to time and especially during emergencies or enemy scares.

With the coming of larger and heavier four-engined bombers the field at Barton Bendish had obviously become inadequate and its days were numbered. To overcome the problem of where

*An aerial view of Downham Market airfield taken in July 1946. Visible along the edges of the main E–W runway can be seen the FIDO installations.* Crown Copyright/MOD. Reproduced with the permission of the Controller of HMSO

to disperse these larger aircraft it was decided to construct an entirely new satellite airfield and for this the shelf of rising land just to the east of Downham Market was chosen. The proposed site was reasonably flat, apart from a slight hump to the north, it was well drained and was largely free of the fogs and mists which tended to gather over the damp Fenlands further west and south. On the debit side was the fact that the site was closely surrounded by villages and was rather too near to Downham Market itself for comfort. Five church towers stood within a mile of the ends of the three proposed runways and there was always going to be a real danger that an aircraft in difficulties might hit one of them or crash onto a built-up area.

The land on which RAF Downham Market was to be built was owned by two estates and was bisected by the Downham to Swaffham road. Most of the land north of the road, where the airfield proper was to be constructed, belonged to R. Cox Farms and was regularly used by the Downham Hunt to pursue foxes. The land south of the road, where eventually the dormitory units were to be built, was owned by the long-established Pratt family of Ryston Hall, near Denver. Large parts of both estates had to be compulsorily purchased before building could begin. In addition, the narrow road which straddled the site of the airfield and linked Crimplesham with Wimbotsham had to be closed and torn up along with all the trees and hedges that bordered the fields.

Construction of the airfield began during the latter part of 1941. It was built at great speed, not with grass tracks as at Marham airfield, but with massive concrete runways. And, instead of the pleasingly designed brick structures which graced pre-war airfields, Bexwell had prefabricated utility buildings of concrete and metal. The main contractor for the work was W. and C. French Ltd, of Buckhurst Hill in Essex. Gravel pits were opened up at Tottenhill, five miles away, and worked continuously to provide the raw materials. For months on end the roads to Downham and Bexwell were like mud tracks as lorries busily transported sand and gravel from the pits to the site where hundreds of Irish navvies laid down the concrete runways. Enormous steel hangars were erected, dozens and dozens of corrugated-steel Nissen huts and concrete-frame offices and workshops were built and miles and miles of underground services were laid. By the spring of 1942 the airfield was largely complete and on 1 April it was formally opened up although many of the buildings and services still needed to be erected or installed.

In February dormitory site No 3, on the road between Bexwell and Ryston Hall, had been finished and RAF personnel started to move in. In the midst of all the comings and goings and frenzied activity there was often much confusion as tremendous efforts were made to get the airfield operational.

*LAC Herbert F. Crisp, 218 Squadron*: I was one of eighteen airmen posted from Pembroke, 962 Balloon Squadron, in February or March 1942 to Marham for work at Downham. The railway warrant was made out to King's Lynn Station and on getting out at Downham Market we were ordered back into the train again and on to King's Lynn to wait there for transport back to Bexwell, where we arrived, in the dark, down a muddy lane near the church. A warrant officer used to visit us from Marham with pay and clothes and fixed up our jobs such as unloading trucks of stores, in fact, everything to fit the 'drome out. In our spare time we had to help digging trenches for cables, with the 'Irishmen', for the runway lighting. As time went on more and more men were posted to the camp and also some women to work in the offices and the cook-house. We were put to doing many different jobs. One of mine was to cycle to Downham post office for the mail. As there was no NAAFI I used to bring cakes and jam tarts back from Stannards for break-time. I also did some hair-cutting, having been a gents' hairdresser in Civvy Street, and was given a picket hut for a shop which I slept in as well.

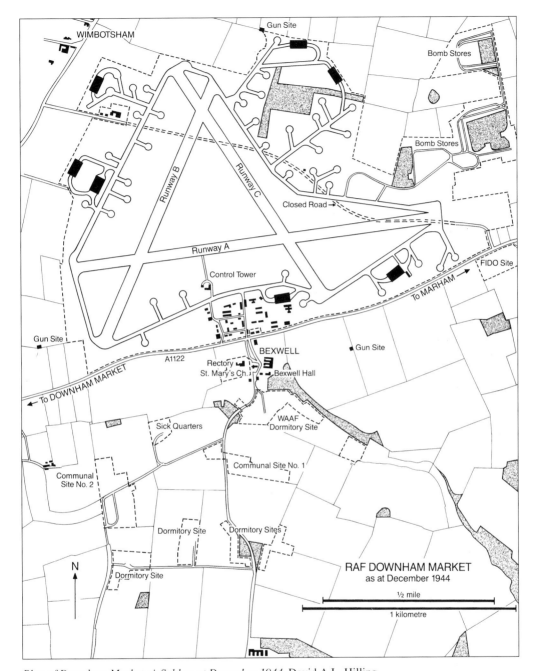

*Plan of Downham Market airfield as at December 1944.* David A.L. Hilling

Entry to the airfield was from the main road and immediately opposite to St Mary's church. Here, clustered around the approach drive, were the station headquarters, crew room and technical sites. The operations block, containing the control tower (also known as the watch office), meteorological office, briefing and interrogation rooms, faced the middle section of the main runway. Outside the control tower there was a signal square where warning rockets could be fired and landing indicators placed.

The layout of the airfield was fairly typical of bomber stations built during the early years of the war, having three concrete runways, each 50 yards wide, laid out to a triangular pattern. The main runway, orientated to take advantage of the prevailing winds, ran parallel to the Swaffham road and was 2,000 yards long; it ended a third of a mile from the then built-up area of Downham Market at one end and a similar distance from Crimplesham village at the other end. A three-mile long perimeter track ran around the whole airfield linking the ends of the three runways to each other and with the dispersal areas and hangars. Between the runways the land was left in rough grass and from May to August each year this green carpet became tinged with bright red poppies. To complete the layout there were thirty-five circular concrete hard-standings where the aircraft dispersed, one to each hard-standing. Altogether enough concrete had been used in the construction of the airfield to make 10 miles of modern motorway!

Dotted around the perimeter track were three large hangars for servicing the aircraft. Two of the hangars were of the standard T2 type and the third was a B1 type intended for civilian repair parties. Later on three more T2 hangars were added for storing gliders. The bomb stores, grouped in neat rows between brick blast walls and covered with green and khaki camouflage netting, were located as far as possible from the camp buildings amongst woods at the north-eastern corner of the airfield.

Ground staff and aircrews lived in Nissen huts on the Bexwell side of the road. The huts were scattered amongst the fields in seven dormitory groups providing accommodation for over two thousand men and women,[2] almost the same population as Downham Market itself. Of this sizable community probably less than 10 per cent comprised aircrew personnel. It was to be some time before all the dormitory groups were completed and it took a long while before the camp reached the capacity for which it was planned. By April aircrews and groundcrews had still not arrived and another two months was to pass before the airfield received its own aircraft. Meanwhile the ground staff continued to move in and prepare the airfield for the bloody contest which, as far as Downham was concerned, had still to commence.

It was during this relatively inactive period that Downham had its first taste of war. It happened on the last-but-one night of May when the historic thousand-bomber raid on Cologne took place. Downham was still not operational but at Marham it was going to be a maximum effort operation. Every available plane at Marham – eighteen Wellingtons of 115 Squadron and nineteen Stirlings of 218 Squadron – was made ready, tested, bombed-up and took off without incident.

Now to get thirty-seven heavily laden aircraft into the air, one after the other, without complications is no easy thing. But that is relatively straightforward compared to landing them all safely at a time when each is short of fuel and many have been shot up and are badly damaged. It was therefore decided that in order to ease the difficulties at Marham, when so many aircraft might be arriving at about the same time, some planes should be allowed to land at the new satellite airfield. There was, apparently, a friendly rivalry between the old established flying control at Marham and its fledgling equivalent at Downham. The senior branch at Marham did its damnedest to bring in all its aircraft as quickly as possible and so prevent any being landed by its junior flying control. In the event, however, the task proved to be too great for the parent station to handle all on its own and three aircraft were landed at Downham. The

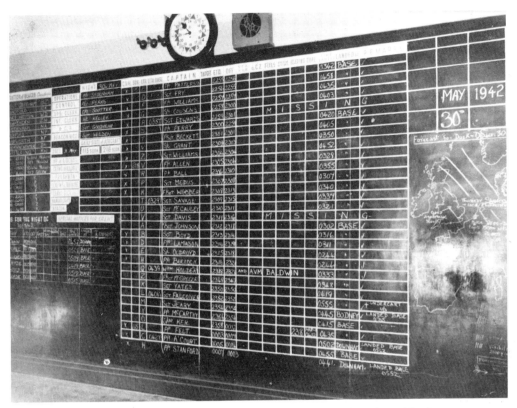

*The Operations Board at Marham on 30 May 1942 for the first thousand-bomber raid – the target Cologne. H-Harry, flown by P/O Stanford, and L-Love, flown by P/O Felt, shown near the bottom of the board were the first operational aircraft to land at Downham Market. L.E. Skan*

first plane, H-Harry, piloted by Pilot Officer Stanford, landed at 4.41 am after a four-and-a-half hour journey.

Thus the new airfield became operational for the first time. It had been quite an effort at Downham even to land three aircraft for the flare-path lighting was not yet working and men were up all night attending to hastily arranged temporary runway lighting while a searchlight was used to 'home-in' the returning planes. The men on duty were rewarded with eggs and bacon, a breakfast usually reserved for aircrew only during the war.

Two nights later, on 1 June, the second thousand-bomber raid took place on Essen. Marham, being a grass airfield, was not the easiest place for the pilots of 218 Squadron to land their Stirlings, which, with their tall, awkward undercarriages, never took happily to the bumpy grass strip. A few Stirlings were still spread-eagled across Marham airfield with collapsed undercarriages when some of 115 Squadron's aircraft returned from the raid and had to be diverted to Downham.

***Sgt Don Bruce, 115 Squadron***: I was stationed at RAF Marham with 115 Squadron. The only time that I was involved with our satellite Downham Market was on 2 June when my pilot and I were sent there to ferry a couple of Wellingtons back to Marham. We took off from Downham Market at 1130 and 1430 to ferry them back to base at Marham. I think that this was the occasion, following the thousand-bomber raid, when three or five Stirlings were spread out on Marham airfield with collapsed undercarts and some 115 Squadron Wimpys were diverted to land at Downham. We went over by road transport to Downham to pick up the Wimpys.

Another incident that took place during this preludial phase was an attack on Downham aerodrome by German raiders. Evidently the German Luftwaffe had a good knowledge of East Anglian airfields for Marham had already been attacked many times and considerable damage and trouble caused there in one way or another. Then, one night in June 1942, it was Downham's turn although at the time of the raid the airfield was still without its own aircraft. Luckily, no damage was done to the airfield but it was a near thing for on the night in question the recently installed runway lighting was switched on and was being tested, one runway at a time. As the enemy aircraft approached the airfield Laurence Skan, the flying control officer, was driving slowly along one of the runways checking that all the flarepath lights were working properly.

**S/Ldr Laurence E. Skan, 218 Squadron**: I was in the middle of one runway when I heard the unmistakable sound of German aircraft. Being well aware that the airfield lights would be visible to the enemy from far away, I sped back as fast as possible to the control tower and slammed the switches off, and almost simultaneously the bombs started coming down. I recall that Group Captain McKee 'phoned to me from Marham hearing the bombs and I was able to give him a running commentary that all (the bombs) were missing the airfield.

In fact, instead of falling on the airfield the bombs fell a mile south-east in a wide scatter around the villages of Crimplesham and West Dereham. I was living with my sister and parents near the airfield at the time and as the bombs whistled down and fell around us we cowered in a deep and over-grown dyke (ditch) at the end of the garden, not minding the stinging nettles and mud until it was all over. Most of the dozen or so 1,000 lb high explosive bombs exploded in open fields making deep craters which eventually filled with water to form ponds.

One bomb, however, landed next to a pair of cottages near Crimplesham church but, fortunately, failed to explode. The main road had to be closed for a few hours while the bomb-disposal squad made the bomb safe and took it away. In addition, hundreds of incendiary bombs were dropped and as these were being extinguished the raiders are said to have machine-gunned the area. The only damage caused by the raid was some broken windows and cracked ceilings in a few houses, while on one farm a bull became frightened by all the noise and tried to escape. On the following Sunday the Reverend Reed held a thanksgiving service in the church to celebrate Crimplesham's safe deliverance.

The squadron earmarked for Downham was the veteran 218 (Gold Coast) Squadron which had been re-formed in 1936 and had, since November 1940, been based at Marham. During 1941 the squadron was 'adopted' by the peoples of the Gold Coast in West Africa. At first the squadron operated with twin-engined Wellington bombers, but from February 1942 the squadron began re-equipping with Short Stirlings, the Royal Air Force's first four-engined heavy bomber, as these gradually became available. While the grass strip at Marham was alright for landing Wellingtons it proved to be less suitable for the huge, four-engined Stirlings. So when Downham became operational the aircrews of 218 Squadron eagerly began to use its concrete runways for practice landings and take-offs in readiness for the forthcoming move. Soon the Stirlings, with their red squadron code letters HA painted on the sides of their fuselages, became a familiar sight on the airfield.

During the first week of July 1942 the squadron started its move to Downham. Groundcrews left Marham with tractors pulling trains of trailers piled up high with engine gantries, tools and accompanying kit along the narrow, twisting country roads. When all the equipment had been transferred the groundcrews settled in to their huts near the dispersals and for the next few months lived rough in their gumboots while the rest of the camp was hurriedly completed. On 7 July 218 Squadron's thirteen Stirlings were flown direct from Marham to Downham Market. By the second week in July the squadron was ready to re-commence operations against the enemy from its new home.

When 218 Squadron moved to Downham the squadron was already under strength. There was no time, however, to wait for much-needed replacements to arrive. For a few days there were air tests and bombing practice flights and then, on 12 July, five days after moving in, operations began. It was a Sunday evening, half an hour after sunset, when M-Mother, piloted by Pilot Officer Farquharsen, took off heavily laden with 9,000 lb of mines on the first operational sortie from Downham Market. There had been no time to install a telephone connection between the flarepath caravan and the control tower so the take-off was laboriously signalled back to the flying control officer with the aid of an aldis lamp. M-Mother was followed five minutes later by R-Robert, piloted by Sergeant Hartley. Together the two planes flew to the Frisian Islands to lay mines off the north-west coast of Germany. It was a comparatively short hop across the North Sea from East Anglia and by two o'clock in the morning the planes had dropped their mines and had both returned safely to the airfield.

The following night three Stirlings took off from Downham on what was to be the first raid from their new base to a target on the German mainland. They joined the Main Force of Wellingtons, Halifaxes and Lancasters from various other squadrons in eastern England and flew on to bomb Duisburg, an industrial town on the edge of the Ruhr coalfield.

Gradually the number of aircraft available for each raid was stepped up over the next fortnight. There were six more raids in July and then the squadron's luck ran out. On 28 July the squadron participated in a raid with the rest of 3 Group and attacked the port of Hamburg in northern Germany. By this time the squadron was sufficiently strong to send twelve aircraft – each loaded with 3 tons of bombs – on the 800-mile, six-hour round trip. The weather was poor as they left the base late at night and it steadily worsened as the planes flew on through the early hours of the morning. Many planes, including three Stirlings from 218 Squadron, had to return home early as a result of weather problems and mechanical defects. The remainder of the force became scattered, but went on to bomb the target as best they could. Less than half the bombers found it. Ironically, the most serious damage of the raid was caused by a direct hit on a hospital.

At a quarter-past-four in the morning the first of 218 Squadron's remaining aircraft returned from Hamburg and landed in the pouring rain. Then over the next hour and a quarter those aircraft that were able to get back landed one by one. But three of 218 Squadron's Stirling aircraft were not able to make it and failed to return from the raid. Amongst them was M-Mother, the first plane to carry out an operation in anger from the airfield at Downham. M-Mother was piloted on this occasion by Squadron Leader Powell.

## CHAPTER 2
# Life on the Camp

**M**ost airmen and airwomen arriving at the airfield for the first time inevitably felt that they were being unceremoniously dumped in a Nissen hut and then left to find their own way round. Finding one's own way around was not easy and it took time. The camp was very large. Being a dispersed camp with multitudes of small buildings spread over many acres, rather than a few big buildings close together as on pre-war airfields, it was easy to get lost. Distances between the dormitory sites, where everyone lived, and other parts of the airfield were considerable and for the ground staff especially it was almost essential to have a bicycle to get around. Otherwise it meant having to get up even earlier in the morning in order to walk to one's place of work and arrive there in time. Some were privileged by their position or job and were able to get a service push-bike immediately; others had to put their names down on a list and then wait for weeks.

When the first squadron arrived in July 1942 conditions on the camp were still primitive. Not all the dormitory sites had been completed and some men needed to be temporarily billeted at the Temperance Hotel in Downham. The hotel's name may have been somewhat off-putting but it did, nevertheless, provide better accommodation than the men would get later at the camp itself where all, except the most senior men and some of the married men who had brought their wives with them, would live in standardized Nissen huts. The Nissen huts were little more than

*F/O McAllister and crew arrive at Downham Market railway station at the start of their tour with 218 Squadron in 1943.* A. Long, via John Reid

corrugated steel structures of semi-circular section bolted on to concrete slabs. They were arranged in seven dormitory groups dispersed amongst the fields and had the uncomfortable disadvantage of being freezing cold in winter and stiflingly hot in summer. Each hut, depending on its length and how it was divided up, held between eight and eighteen men or women. In the centre of each hut there was a round, coal-burning stove which was intended to give a general heat throughout the hut. Unfortunately the stoves were difficult to light, almost impossible to keep going once lit and, unless one was within spitting distance of it, seemed to make no apparent difference to the outside temperature.

While the conditions in the huts were bad enough there were times when even the basic amenities of life were in short supply. During the summer of 1944, for instance, when there was a water shortage due to a faulty pump baths were prohibited and toilets could only be flushed once a day!

**Peggy Moorcroft (nee Sgt 'Tommy' Thompson), WAAF**: During this time we were not allowed to have a bath and could only have one cup of tea per meal. It was no good taking a large mug as the tea was dished out of a pail with a ladle and one ladleful per person was the ration. I can remember filling a cocoa tin with water and putting it on the hut stove to get a little warm water to wash.

Scattered among the fields, along the lanes behind St Mary's church and Bexwell Hall, were five dormitory sites for non-commissioned men and two large communal sites which contained all the 'public' buildings such as canteens, institute, stores, post office, education block, gymnasium and chapel. Officers were accommodated on a separate dormitory site at the rear of the Rectory. There was also a small hospital standing in the middle of a field and isolated from the rest of the camp buildings. The women of the Women's Auxiliary Air Force (WAAF) lived on a separate dormitory site nearer the church complete with its own mess rooms and institute. Curiously, while the men were reasonably well equipped with toilets – at the rate of one latrine block to every three Nissen huts – the WAAF site only had three latrine blocks to share between twenty-seven huts! Consequently the women had generally to walk further to get to their toilets and thus going there in the dark late at night could be a rather trying experience. On their way back to their huts from the airfield proper the women, like the men, needed to pass the ancient church. This could be scary at times.

**Peggy Moorcroft (nee Sgt 'Tommy' Thompson), WAAF**: There was a man whom I used to see when I came back from duty in the Ops Block at night. He would be standing outside the church shouting 'Repent ye, repent ye.' I can't remember what he looked like except that he wore canvas shoes. One night we opened our hut door and he was just outside. We wondered if he was a spy – probably some harmless old local character.

For most people on the camp the day started very early. Carrying all their bits and pieces in 'goon-bags' the men set out from their billets in the chilly dawn air and made for the open-sided 'ablutions' block where they washed and shaved at a row of tin wash-hand basins. According to LAC Bill Overton, 218 Squadron, 'there were hot and cold water taps, but unless you were up with the lark the hot water was usually cold.'

Then armed with mug and 'irons' the men went across to the cook-house for breakfast. After standing in a long, shuffling queue for ages the amount of food doled out never seemed to be enough. It was not particularly appetizing or filling but was, for the most part, nutritious; at least, no one ever starved there.

*W/Cdr Peter McDermott, DFC, DFM, 608 Squadron*: The food, within the restrictions of war-time rationing, was good and carefully supervised by Doc, the Group aviation medico, a wing commander who occasionally flew on Pathfinder 'ops' in a Lanc. Grilled steak and egg were standard before 'ops' – nothing which could cause wind! Woe betide the catering officer who fell down in this respect and was discovered by the Doc.

Perhaps the standard of food had improved during the course of the war, for not everyone shared such an understanding view of the fare.

*LAC Len Warner, 218 and 623 Squadrons*: It was not long before I found that the food at Bexwell was of terrible quality. We all kept complaining about it until one day we decided to do something. The camp mascot, Pilot Officer Prune, a mongrel of many varieties, was well-fed for a few days and then, by arrangement, we all went to lunch at the same time on the appointed day. In comes the Duty Officer. 'Any complaints?' he asked. Out stepped the poor bod who had drawn the paper marked X in the draw. 'Yes sir,' he said; 'the food isn't fit for a dog to eat.' 'Well, we'll see,' replied the officer and he instructed the bod to put his lunch plate on the floor. The dog was brought in, took one sniff at the plate and walked off. Little did the Duty Officer know that we had added paraffin to the plate!

Bread was the only kind of food in reasonable abundance. There was always a big bin in the canteen which contained off-cuts of loaves or stale rounds of bread and it was usual, in winter, after the evening meal, to take pieces back to the billet to toast on the stove. Sometimes the toast would be supplemented by eggs not so innocently 'discovered' in the hen-house of some isolated farm.

Good health was important, especially for aircrews, although conditions on the camp were not always conducive to its continuance.

*P/O Reg Davey, 218 Squadron*: Apart from various nervous and stomach disorders aircrew were liable to suffer ear, throat and sinus infections from flying in noisy, draughty and poorly heated aircraft at sub-zero temperatures. Few men reported sick with these complaints for there was the great fear that they would be 'grounded', miss operations and then have to complete extra trips with a strange and, maybe, inexperienced crew. The glamour of operational flying soon wore off and there set in a strong personal desire to remain fit and see the end of the war. This required action at both physical and psychological levels. At Downham Market in 1943 those of us who had previously cheerfully dropped out of Church Parades along with 'Jews and Atheists' very soon stayed for the Services and eagerly sought out the company of the overworked Padre. Our night-time escape exercises across the Fens came to be treated more seriously despite being hunted by a very keen Home Guard Company. Many flew with good luck charms ranging from St Christopher medals to girl friends' most intimate garments. Sometimes they worked, sometimes, sadly, they didn't. Considering war-time rationing the food we got was good but we crammed ourselves with cod-liver oil capsules freely supplied at meal times; they may have done some good in keeping away colds but the oil played havoc with our digestions! In this situation we were sitting targets for the Messing Sergeant to cash in and put on sale various items to improve our health. On one occasion he purchased a large consignment of Andrew's Liver Salts and spread the word that they would flush our jaded systems and 'put us on top of the world.' We each bought a large tin but soon found that, combined with food such as baked beans, we were not very nice people to fly with and it was the toilet rather than the world we were on top of!

*Bexwell Hall in 1943.* L.E. Skan

Recreational facilities at the camp were, at first, limited to the NAAFI where one could get a beer or play snooker, table tennis or darts. Later, when the camp became larger, the original Sergeants' Mess was converted into a kind of theatre where films were shown and ENSA occasionally came to put on a show. Most of the time, however, the men were too exhausted to go out and much of their very limited spare time was spent just lying on the bed or playing cards in the hut. There were, of course, dances at the NAAFI and the Sergeants' Mess and also occasional parties. The station had its own small band which was led by Corporal Sam Costa, who also sang and later became famous as a band leader on the radio. When the band went on parade the big drum was taken on a platform carried on old pram wheels with Corporal Costa leading the way and the rest of the band following behind.

The Sergeants' Mess dances were often pretty wild affairs which tended to get rougher and deeper in beer-swill as the night progressed. In later years, when there were two squadrons stationed on the airfield, if one was not able to give the expected answer to a question about which squadron one belonged to then there was a good chance of having your tie chopped off just below the knot! When a party was being organized sugar and fat rations were cut back for weeks ahead of the event so that the mess-cook (one of whom was said to have been the chef before the war at London's Grosvenor Hotel) had sufficient ingredients to prepare buffets equal to the occasion. For these happenings local personalities were invited; more importantly nurses – as many as possible, and often from hospitals as far away as King's Lynn and Ely – were asked to go along to swell the ranks of the womenfolk.

Winters on the airfield at Downham Market were usually very cold and miserable and, being so near the low-lying Fens, fog was a common occurrence. How to heat the huts adequately was a cause of considerable concern for their occupants for the official allocation of coke was meagre in the extreme. Finding sufficient fuel was always a problem and a fair amount of unofficial coppicing of trees in the surrounding countryside went on from time to time in attempts to keep the home fires burning.

*Aircrew and groundcrew in front of their Stirling III (B-Baker) of 623 Squadron, late 1943.* R.B. Belderson

**F/O B.J. Sherry, DFC, 608 Squadron**: We seemed to be constantly scrounging for fuel for the little stoves. I remember one cold, winter day when a Fairy Godmother in the form of the GPO arrived and dug a hole in the lane outside our billet and deposited a telegraph pole alongside it. Someone acquired a double-handed saw and, once dusk had fallen, the pole was rapidly sawn up and spirited through the hedge in sections to be chopped up and cached. Tree branches were used to sweep the lane free of sawdust and we sat tight to see what would happen. After about ten days another pole was deposited beside the hole. Once darkness had fallen the rasp of the saw was heard, all traces of sawdust removed and by morning the second pole had mysteriously vanished. Unfortunately, the GPO did not fall for it a third time. A fortnight later they brought the pole, planted it and wired it up all in one day. However, we had not done badly and the kerosene-coated pine burned beautifully and kept the stove going for a number of weeks.

**F/Sgt Paddy Cronin, 635 Squadron**: The winter of 1944 was so cold that we were always short of wood. Colonel Pratt's bullock sheds down the lane had some lovely wood on them and as some of the boards were loose we helped them off. The Colonel went to complain to the Group Captain and asked him to stop his men taking the wood. Group said 'yes, of course I will see to it.' But he could not do anything; we were here today and maybe gone tomorrow. And we could not have cared less! Once we heard that he had complained it only encouraged us to take more, so eventually there was not a lot left of the sheds.

The limited heat from the stoves in the Nissen huts did little to keep out the damp. The metal construction of the huts attracted condensation and any clothes, such as pyjamas, left to air in front of the stoves before going to bed soon filled the place with steam. Often it was necessary to sweep up the water from under the bed before retiring to sleep. Also, in order to sleep comfortably it was, according to some of the temporary residents, almost obligatory to 'dress up' in multiple layers of clothing including, when available, flying kit. Strangely, it was the Canadians who seemed to complain most although they were supposed to be used to the cold. It was probably the damp air and lack of central heating which upset them for they were said to be always going on about 'this Goddam climate'.

*F/O B.J. Sherry, DFC*: There was one Canadian character whose preparations for bed had to be seen to be believed. Anyone who went on leave had his blankets borrowed by this chap who created a blanket cocoon of his own. Next, water was boiled on the stove for a hot-water bottle which he put in to pre-heat his cocoon. He then proceeded to dress for bed . . . aircrew underwear, two or three pairs of pyjamas, long flying socks, aircrew sweater and Balaclava helmet. When ready for bed he looked like Captain Oates preparing to walk out into the Antarctic night. He, however, had no intention of stirring any further from the stove than was strictly necessary, and finally, when he was satisfied that his nest was properly aired, he used to burrow in from the bottom of his bed, having previously arranged for someone to tuck in his entrance opening. No part of him was visible and how he didn't asphyxiate during the night I'll never know! Next morning, with the stove out and the hut cooled down he used to emerge from his blanket cocoon and shave in the tepid water from his hot-water bottle.

Generally winter evenings were spent around the stove reading, writing or playing cards. There was usually little incentive to go out. The majority, after working long hours on duty with little chance of any rest, felt shattered and were inclined to 'stay at home'.

Some improvements were made to the Officers' Mess late in 1944 in readiness for Christmas that year. In particular it was decided that the Mess should have a proper bar. With this in mind walls were knocked down between two of the rooms and a passage and soon a respectable bar, with mural decorations by WAAF Sergeant R.M. Vaughan, resulted. The bar, known as the Fingerwell Inn, was opened with appropriate celebrations.

Meanwhile the ante-room to the Officers' Mess had become something of an ice box during that unusually cold winter. Fortunately, the problem was overcome by an ingenious device which had been suggested by one of the engineering officers, Flight Lieutenant Pringle, for converting the big coke stove to an oil-water fuel system by using thick waste oil from the aero-engines of the aircraft. When the conversion was completed waste oil and water were piped through separate taps to the top of the stove and were allowed to slowly drip down on to a pre-heated brick at the base of the stove. The brick had to be initially heated by a blow-lamp to a sufficiently high temperature to vaporize the oil but after that it was self-sustaining and the stove continued to glow a dull red with apparently nothing inside save a red-hot brick. The stove-pipe gave out a deep throated roar like a waterfall while the stove itself had an alarming propensity to belch out smoke and flame at unexpected moments. But it worked and, because of its likeness to the fearsome German V1 flying-bomb and the V2 rocket, it was immediately christened the 'V3'.

Christmas Day was the only day in the calendar when no aircraft operations were ever launched and this brought some relaxation in the tempo of work. For those staying on in the camp there was an early morning carol service and a special Christmas dinner. Officers and NCOs served the 'other ranks' at dinner in keeping with RAF tradition. As many of the officers and NCOs had already started to celebrate their 'waiting' was not necessarily of the highest quality but was often accompanied by the splash of spilling soup, the fumes of liquor and the noise of breaking dishes. The menu hardly varied from Christmas to Christmas. In 1942 there was cream of tomato soup followed by roast turkey, roast pork, apple sauce and roast and boiled

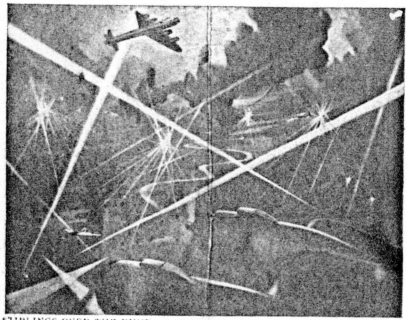

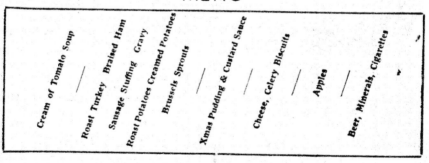

*Menu for Christmas dinner at the airfield in 1943. Lowestoft-born artist David Smith served in the RAF and made a number of operational trips over Germany in order to gather material for his pictorial records. H.F. Crisp*

potatoes. For dessert there was Christmas pudding and sherry sauce followed by mince pies, beer, minerals and cigarettes. In 1943 the menu was the same except that braised ham was offered in place of pork and the sherry sauce had been replaced by custard sauce. All ranks joined in the singing of traditional songs and then the officers and NCOs did the washing up. Back in their huts after the dinner the 'other ranks' warmed themselves up by mulling beer with the aid of red-hot pokers heated in the stove.

For some of the men from the Commonwealth countries stationed at the airfield, such as the Ghanaians with 218 Squadron, the strangest sight of winter must have been the snow. And there was plenty of snow! The winter of 1944/45, in particular, was especially harsh. Christmas 1944 was the coldest there had been since the beginning of the war, with temperatures down to –10° C, and in January 1945 there were unusually heavy falls of snow. Members of all sections of the camp, including WAAFs, paraded each day on the main runway armed with shovels and were then set to work alongside the snow-ploughs endeavouring to ensure that the airfield remained serviceable. In addition to clearing the runways the men and women fought numerous snowball battles and erected many snow-men and snow-women. For many of the Australians on the camp at that time it was their first sight of snow and they made the most of the fun and rushed out to take photographs to send back home.

Life on the airfield had plenty of 'downs' as well as 'ups'. But there was little point in being depressed about the difficulties or being morbid about the losses any longer than necessary. For many servicemen and women these were, in fact, exciting, happy days.

*Eleanor Zaleski (nee Cpl Bignall), WAAF*: Downham Market was undoubtedly the happiest Station I stayed on during my five years of service. We had lovely dances in the NAAFI and I guess we just all lived for that day or night, as I suppose everyone did in those days.

It was even more important for the aircrews that the station should be a happy place. For them it was a matter of life or death whether or not they completed their tours and a happy crew without unnecessary problems on their minds probably had a better chance of getting through than an unhappy crew. In the main the crews were very young and would have, in normal life, much to look forward to. Often they were irrepressibly exuberant and were frequently boisterous. The constant dance with death did little to kill their joy of life; for some, indeed, it may have enhanced it.

When 218 Squadron departed at the end of February 1944 its place was soon taken, in March, by the 'old hands' of 635 Squadron. Most of these crews were on their second tour but were still as full of life as ever. 635 Squadron was, in fact, a new squadron formed from flights of 35 Squadron based at Graveley in Huntingdonshire and 97 Squadron based at Bourn, near Cambridge. Though experienced veterans of the air war the new crews had lost nothing of their inveterate good humour and independent ways.

*F/Sgt William D. Ogilvie, 635 Squadron*: When we, the C flight of 97 Squadron, left Bourn to fly to Downham we were under strict orders *not* to 'shoot up' either airfield. But we were in high spirits. Some of us were not very happy about the new Squadron Commander of 97. Too much 'pep talk' and exhortation to 'do better' to an all-volunteer and pretty well seasoned Squadron; and we knew the score and kept our silence. Needless to say we 'shot up' both aerodromes, and flew in loose V formation, leaving the navigation to others; but no one was actually navigating. The skipper asked for a fix. Ron said the new 'drome was on one side somewhere. I spotted it. The skipper called up the others on the RT and we went down for a low pass. Our low pass 'blew over' two, waving Land Army girls.

*Men and women of the Motor Transport section at the Christmas party held in Denver village hall, 1944.* P. Dunthorne, via John Reid

Two stories connected with the airfield evoke something of the spirit of those days. The first story concerns 635 Squadron. Normally aircrew did not take part in parades, but on one occasion a certain warrant officer decided to hold a parade because he was dissatisfied with the men's attitude and wanted to take them in hand. The men were lazy, according to the warrant officer, and he thought that they badly needed smartening up. The night before the planned parade some of the men chatted up the warrant officer in the bar and kept plying him with drinks until eventually he got drunk. When he was out for the count they locked him up in a spare room to sleep it off. Next morning some men went on parade and some did not. When the Wing Commander and Adjutant arrived for the parade there was no sign of the warrant officer. 'Where's the W/O?' the Wing Commander asked. 'Don't know,' was the reply from the men. 'Well, we can't have a parade without the W/O!' So the parade was immediately dismissed, much to the satisfaction of the men.

635 Squadron flew four-engined Lancasters. In August 1944 the squadron was joined by a new squadron, number 608, which flew the smaller but much faster twin-engined Mosquitos. The officers of the two squadrons shared the same Mess and although there were friendships between individual members of the two squadrons they did not, on the whole, fraternize very much with each other but tended to keep themselves to themselves. Usually it was 608 Squadron in the Bar while 635 Squadron occupied the Lounge. The second story concerns 608 Squadron.

One night Pete, a Dutch pilot flying with the squadron, landed after an operation over Germany and, not noticing that the entrance indicator was un-illuminated, turned his Mosquito into its usual dispersal point. Unfortunately there were two aircraft already parked on the hard-standing and the arrival of the third Mosquito was marked by a series of loud, crunching sounds as it collided into them. A few nights after that incident the squadron decided to celebrate some awards that it had received and took a 'liberty' bus and went to a pub in the countryside. The squadron commander and two flight commanders followed in a car but on the way there they saw a couple of dimmed lights in front of them. 'Let's scare the shit out of those cyclists by going in between them,' one of the commanders suggested. But the lights that they had seen were not those of cyclists but the heavily shielded side-lights of a petrol tanker! The car was damaged but, luckily, not its occupants, and so the party continued on its way. Later, when all had returned to the Mess, the men decided to have a sing-song. After having first ensured that there were no WAAF officers left in the Mess they raised their voices and began singing RAF songs of all kinds. Suddenly a door opened and in walks the station commander followed by a gaggle of 635 Squadron officers. Everyone assumed that the 635 men were going to join the 608 men, but the station commander had other ideas.

'I will not have filthy songs sung in my mess,' he yelled.

The 608 officers bowed stiffly and then they all calmly walked out. Next morning there was a 608 Squadron briefing.

'This is a bloody fine squadron, I must say,' began their squadron commander. 'First, one of our pilots, by a stupid, unavoidable accident, damages three of our own aircraft; then someone else manages to write off a car; and to finish it all off, a gang of my officers insults the station commander in the Mess. Now some of these things are forgivable but the unavoidable aircraft accident certainly is not.'

Everyone stayed quiet, except Pete who, though Dutch, fancied his command of English.

'But sir,' the Dutchman said, 'if the accident was unavoidable, surely it couldn't be stopped.'

'That's the trouble with you bloody foreigners,' the squadron commander retorted, 'you just can't understand simple English!'

From time to time various VIPs visited the airfield. The first of these very important persons to show up at Downham was the Duke of Kent. He paid a visit on 29 July 1942, soon after the airfield had become fully operational. It was noted in the Squadron Operations Record Book[3] that 'the Duke showed a keen interest in the groundcrew staff and spoke with several of them. He saw one of our Stirlings bombed up and toured the aerodrome generally, completing his tour by a visit to the Officers' Mess.' The visit was marred, unfortunately, by 218 Squadron's first loss from its new home when three Stirlings – out of twelve sent out on operations the previous night – failed to return after being shot down.

The King and Queen visited the airfield on 26 May the following year and held an investiture ceremony in Bexwell Hall. A number of men from 218 Squadron were decorated at the Investiture. But for some of the rank and file the royal visit was not so exciting and is remembered for the long hours spent standing and waiting while the King and Queen were shown around.

**Cpl H.W.S. Gable, Motor Transport**: A special tea was laid on for some of the lucky ones, but we had our tea at a later time as we had to stand outside the gates and, as the royal party left the 'drome, throw our hats in the air and cheer like mad! When we arrived at the mess our tea was down to earth as usual.

During 1943 Downham Market also hosted a visit of the Brazilian Air Mission while it was on a fact-finding tour of Britain. The visit took place on 18 November and included seeing one of the squadron's Stirlings being bombed-up and listening in to the interrogation of aircrews on return from an operational raid.

Another royal visitor was the Duke of Gloucester who came to see what was going on early in 1944. According to one journalist, writing later of the event, 12 February 'was a sunny, but cold morning. While we were following the Duke around on his tour some fires attracted our

*King George VI and Queen Elizabeth leave Bexwell Hall after their visit to RAF Downham Market in May 1943.* Downham Market Town Council, via M.S. Bullen

*Members of the Brazilian Mission with G/Capt H.H. Downs, AFC, in front of a Stirling III (E-Easy) of 218 Squadron in November 1943.* Imperial War Museum (IWM) CH11648

attention. At first they looked like twitch fires. Then we saw these groups of fires link up, and finally there was a wall of flame lining each side of the runway a mile or more long.'[4] This phenomenon was, of course, the fog dispersal system (FIDO) being demonstrated. FIDO, which was an acronym for Fog Intensive Dispersal Operation, consisted of long pipelines, drilled with holes at regular intervals and pointing upwards, on either side of the main runway which, when lit, burned vaporized petrol, blow-light fashion. It burned with maximum heat and minimum smoke, the warmed air lifting the fog and thus ensuring a tunnel of clear air just above the runway.

**S/Ldr Laurence E. Skan, 218 Squadron**: I gathered that it was a somewhat awesome experience to land an aircraft under those conditions. It was a fantastic sight, like something out of Dante's *Inferno*, and the first time FIDO was lit we had telephone calls from many miles away (I believe one even came from Peterborough) to ask if we were on fire!

FIDO was installed at Downham Market in September 1943 and was only the second airfield to be equipped with this strange device. The first trial burn took place in October while tests using aircraft were made the following month. During the latter part of November the fog settled in and persisted for several days. Under these ideal test conditions Wing Commander John Wooldridge, the Aeronautical Adviser to the Petroleum Warfare Department, made a landing in an Airspeed Oxford. He reported that:

At 1600 hours on November 21, 1943, the test aircraft took off from RAF Feltwell and set course for RAF Downham Market, where a specimen landing was to be attempted. The

*The visit of HRH the Duke of Gloucester to the airfield in February 1944. With the Duke (at the foot of steps to the Operations Block) are Air Vice Marshal Harrison, the Officer Commanding 3 Group, and G/Capt H.H. Downs, AFC, the Station Commander. L.E. Skan*

ground was obscured immediately after take-off and the fog bank eventually cleared between 300 and 400 feet. The aircraft set course for Downham, flying solely on instruments, and the Downham beam was picked up successfully shortly after take-off. So bad were general conditions, however, that the lighted burners were not seen until the aircraft was flying at 1,500 feet across the aerodrome and they first appeared as a considerable diffused red glow. By the time we were directly overhead, the plan of the burners could be seen quite clearly through the intervening mist and low cloud. Normal beam approach procedure was carried out, with the aircraft again flying in completely blind conditions until it reached a point almost 1,000 yards from the beginning of the runway. From that point on, the burners became progressively more visible and the pilot was able to 'line up' his aircraft by looking out ahead and a satisfactory landing was made.[5]

FIDO was mainly used to land aircraft during very poor weather and in emergencies. Occasionally it was also used to assist take-offs in poor weather when it was essential that the raid had to be mounted at almost any cost as, for example, at the time of the German offensive in the Ardennes in December 1944 (see page 81). Altogether FIDO was used operationally at Downham Market on at least thirteen occasions to land 161 aircraft and to assist 36 aircraft taking off.

Not all visits to the airfield were planned beforehand. One interesting surprise visit happened early on a foggy morning at the end of November 1944 when a United States Army Douglas Skymaster landed with fifteen passengers, including a general, two brigadiers, a foreign correspondent of the *New York Times* and a nurse. The plane had been on a transatlantic flight from the Azores to Prestwick, Scotland and had been flying in cloud all the time. Flying conditions were abominable, there being virtually no visual aids to help navigation, and, moreover, it had been impossible to make any radio contacts. After many hours flying on 'dead reckoning' courses there was a break in the clouds and the navigator was able to get an astro-fix on the moon. The pilot, however, was not at all amused when he discovered that not only had they unknowingly flown right across Britain but that the plane was now out over the North Sea and well on its way to German occupied territory.

Turning the airplane around, and with fuel running low, the pilot flew back on a reciprocal course. At 6.30 am the quiet sky over Downham Market was suddenly shattered by the roar of the Skymaster's engines. It was obvious to those on the ground that the plane was going to try to land although the cloud base was only 500 feet and there was going to be no time to clear the fog by igniting FIDO. Amidst a series of alarming roars and splutters the pilot managed somehow to get the giant plane safely down. He then taxied it in before the fuel finally gave out. So confused were the crew of the Skymaster that they weren't sure whether they had landed in friendly or hostile territory and when they stepped down from the plane it was with their revolvers drawn at the ready.

Engineless gliders were visitors of a different kind. During the first six months of 1943, but mostly in March, some twenty-six Airspeed Horsa gliders were delivered to the airfield to be stored there until required for the invasion of France. Each glider was nearly as large as a four-engined Lancaster bomber and consequently they took up a considerable amount of valuable space.

Most of the gliders were taken away again on 10 March 1944, during the quiet period between the departure of 218 Squadron and the arrival of 635 Squadron. They eventually took part in the invasion of Normandy on D-Day. The wings and fuselages of the gliders had been painted with white stripes and when the Albemarles towed them into the air it looked as though a mini-invasion was about to take place. One glider managed to accidentally slip its tow-rope

*A Horsa glider takes off towed by an Albemarle. Horsa gliders, painted with white D-Day stripes, were stored at the airfield during 1943 and early 1944.* IWM CH12963

and came down in a field at Stradsett a mile or so from the airfield. I managed to go and see the grounded glider with my father but by the time we arrived at the site there was already an armed guard standing by the stricken aircraft and we were allowed no nearer than the boundary hedge.

The remaining six Horsas were despatched in April and went, first to Hawarden in northern Wales and then to Birkenhead where they were transported by ship to Sicily for the invasion of the Italian mainland.

From time to time there were other, less welcome, visitors: namely German intruder aircraft; but of these dangerous visitors more in a later chapter.

# CHAPTER 3
# Beyond the Airfield

Fighting a war every night over enemy territory while relaxing by day in England was unlike any other kind of existence. It took an enormous psychological toll, but it had some compensations.

*F/O B.J. Sherry, DFC, 608 Squadron*: Bomber aircrews, raiding over Occupied Europe, led a strangely schizophrenic existence. By day, in the quiet English countryside; by night, engaged in a running fight in the cold and dark over enemy territory; and then coming back from this bad dream to the calm of the Fenlands. It was two totally different worlds that we moved between. If the dark side could be a hell, then daytime, largely by contrast, became a bit of a heaven. Morning came, you were still alive, and very conscious of being alive. Everything tasted better . . . jokes were funnier . . . colours were brighter . . . birdsong was sweeter . . . nature lovelier . . . all girls were beautiful. There was a heightened intensity about the daytime half of the equation as well as the night-time part, and very little excuse was needed to have a celebration. The unspoken reason was that we were still here, still in the land of the living. We had some memorable parties, both on the station and in the pubs of the surrounding villages, and enjoyed some marvellous hospitality from the local people.

Although the camp was in some ways like a small town, with many of the facilities enjoyed in such a place, there was, nevertheless, always a tremendous urge to get off the airfield whenever there was any free time, and to go into Downham, King's Lynn or one of the nearby villages. The usual way of getting away was to hop on a bicycle. If one didn't have a bike on joining the station then one had to go on a waiting list for a few weeks until one became available. Tradesmen got priority so that they could chase around the airfield to carry out their various duties.

Downham Market was just a few minutes away from the camp on a bicycle, and it didn't take very long for the airmen and airwomen to get to know the place. Bicycles could be stored at various garages and yards in the town for two *old* pence. These 'parking lots' were almost essential for although everyone needed a bike at some time they were in short supply and any bicycle left unattended was soon stolen. On average five bicycles a week were lost and reported to the Downham police.

Downham lay just over a mile from the airfield entrance. It was situated on a shelf of land overlooking the Great Ouse and beyond stretched the uncompromisingly flat Fens. It was, and still is, a charming little town full of architectural interest. Mostly built of mellow, coffee-coloured carstone and pale yellow brick, it has a good thirteenth-century church on the hill and a quaint, late nineteenth-century cast-iron clock tower in the Market Square where the main streets meet. The continuous facades of both High Street and Bridge Street are punctuated by many arched openings leading to alleyways reaching far back.

With a population of only three thousand Downham didn't seem to have, on the face of things, a lot to offer the war-weary. Yet the men and women from the airfield found many reasons to visit the town. For some, the first thing to do after arriving at the aerodrome was to attend one of the churches or chapels in Downham and chat up members of the congregation in order to meet local people and get a feel of the atmosphere of the place. Sometimes, a visit to

*Downham Market in the 1940s showing the Market Square and High Street. The shop awning on the left-hand side of High Street marks the position of Sly's Café.* Mike Bullen Collection

Downham was merely a trip to Stannard's shop, at the foot of the hill on the way in to the town from the airfield, to buy cigarettes and cakes. At other times the reason might be to get a cup of tea or a meal in surroundings different to those on the camp. The WVS canteen in the Town Hall was popular and always did a good service.

Sly's Café, in High Street, was a favourite amongst aircrews; especially after missing breakfast in the Mess – a not uncommon event due to late returns from raids.

*Sgt Maxie Booth, 218 Squadron*: I remember getting up late after being on 'ops' most of the night and cycling down to Sly's for breakfast. There was usually a whole gaggle of aircrews doing the same. In due course the Station Police would arrive to turf us out and get us back to the station, often for another briefing for the next 'op'.

Not all went to Sly's Café, for each crew had its own preferred meeting place.

*Sgt Pat Nolan, 635 Squadron*: Another custom our particular crew indulged in was that after crew assembly, if we were not on a training exercise, the skipper would ring up the Temperance Hotel and we would cycle down for a breakfast of ham and eggs. There was no shortage of these two commodities in Norfolk. The cost was two shillings and sixpence!

All the pubs and clubs in Downham and in the surrounding villages were frequently visited by men and women from the airfield.

*Mrs J. Pointer (nee Smith), WAAF*: On our off-duty days we would cycle over to Denver, past the Mill, and on to Jenyn's Arms where you could always obtain some refreshment. This was a favourite, ranking alongside Sly's Café and the Crown.[6]

Of Downham's hostelries the best known and most popular was the eighteenth-century Crown Hotel in Bridge Street, where Mr and Mrs Crump held sway, 'fathering' and 'mothering' the incredibly young airmen when they called in on off-duty nights. Beer was served through a small hatch and because of the sudden increase in business following the airfield's construction the Crumps' own front room had been opened up to provide additional space. The Crown became a kind of unofficial rest-centre for the squadrons and often there would be food for the men at closing time to send them on their ways.

The Castle Hotel, another eighteenth-century hospice, was more fashionable and tended to be used by the higher ranks. It specialized in providing accommodation for the airmen's wives when they were able to visit their husbands during stand-down periods.

Many of the village pubs were ideal for a quiet evening with a few pints, a game of shove-ha'penny and a natter with friends and colleagues. But each pub was different and had its own character and adherents. At the Jolly Waterman a dear lady entertained on the piano, while at another pub, according to Sgt Pat Nolan, 'a blonde WAAF transport driver used to sit at the piano with a pint of beer and sing operatic arias.' The Hare, on the King's Lynn road just beyond the airfield perimeter, was run by 'Bill', the wife of the landlord, while he was serving in Coastal Command searching for aircrew who had come down in the North Sea.

A visit to the pub was a chance to relax and, perhaps, let one's hair down a bit.

*S/Ldr G.M. Rothwell, 218 Squadron*: One evening we went to the local pub in the Morris Flight van. On the return journey I had difficulty in seeing what was ahead as the headlights were covered with the customary slotted hood to conform with blackout regulations. The narrow footpath from Downham Market to the airfield was crowded with returning airmen and women in varying stages of intoxication and spilling over on to the road. I felt a bump but did not appreciate that anything untoward had occurred until some time later when we were in the anteroom enjoying a nightcap. The WAAF Flight Officer came storming in and told me I had knocked over her oldest WAAF for whom she had a high regard and affection. I was very concerned but it turned out that the Flight Officer's indignation was due to the fact that when the side of the flight van had bumped the WAAF's shoulder she had stumbled and her false teeth had shot out of her mouth and shattered on the ground. To make matters worse, we were expecting a visit from the King and Queen and it was planned to present to their Majesties the oldest WAAF on the station: it was problematic whether the poor woman could be fitted with a new set of teeth for the big occasion.

On another occasion when we had been to a local hostelry and were returning late at night we decided to raid the Group Captain's asparagus beds. We climbed the stone wall into the garden and were busy pulling up the spears when the shutters on the first floor of the house flew open and there was the irate CO in his pyjamas able to see clearly in the bright moonlight what we were doing. We took to our heels, hoping we had managed to avoid being identified. No such luck, as I was summoned to appear before the CO next day together with the Senior Medical Officer. The Group Captain then waded into me and told me that I was a disgrace and that if anything went wrong in the neighbourhood such as a WAAF being knocked down or a pub being set on fire he had only to look as far as Rothwell and his crew to discover the culprits. He then turned to the doctor and said he was surprised to find that he had been involved in the escapade, whereupon the doctor protested most indignantly his innocence and that he had been asleep in his bed. Then I realized how the confusion had occurred. One of our party, whose initials were D.R., was always known as 'Doc'. Obviously the CO had heard us calling out to him during our foray into the asparagus beds and had assumed that the medical officer was one of our party.

Often the drinking was boisterous. 608 Squadron, for instance, had a Welfare Fund (to which all contributed) which though intended for the purchase of amenities went mainly on a tremendous party every month or so when there was a stand-down. First, there would be a football match in the afternoon between aircrews and groundcrews, with the groundcrews usually having the edge. Then, in the evening, the Squadron Commanding Officer, Wing Commander R.C. Alabaster, would take the crews down to a pub in Stow Bardolph in a five-ton truck for an all-ranks booze-up. Not surprisingly, the squadron became affectionately known as 'Alabaster's Forty Thieves'. The Wing Commander himself led his men in singing a party-piece known as 'Sending up the Rocket'.

During the summer of 1944 635 Squadron were involved in many tactical support operations over the Normandy beach-heads. These operations often entailed early morning take-offs and everything possible was done to ensure success, including getting up in time for the operation.

**Sgt Pat Nolan**: There seemed to be an unwritten but recognized procedure that the pubs in Downham would put the towels up at about 9 pm. The Station Master assisted by the Padre would make their rounds and chase aircrews back to base. No doubt after we retired from the scene the remaining clientele continued their activities.

In addition to pubs Downham offered the 'pictures' and frequent dances. The Regent Cinema, in High Street, changed its programmes twice a week and had two performances of 'pictures' on Saturdays. Many of the films were overtly patriotic and some, such as those about the air war, simply reflected the life the service men and women were already leading. *One of Our Aircraft is Missing*, for instance, which was shown at the Regent in September 1942, had been filmed a few miles away at Marham in the previous year.

*Downham Market in the 1940s with the cast-iron Clock Tower, built in 1878, visible in the foreground.*
*The building on the right-hand side is the Town Hall where dances were held twice weekly during the war.*
Mike Bullen Collection

Dances were held twice a week at the Town Hall overlooking the Market Square. The little dance hall at Denver – where a chocolate cake was auctioned every Saturday night – was also much frequented, partly on account of the fact that it was easy to get to by going down the back lane from the dormitory areas and thus avoiding passing the guards.

**F/Sgt Wally H. Hitchcock, DFM, 635 Squadron**: At Downham we played table tennis in the chapel rooms. We either walked or cycled everywhere, and often visited Denver, Hilgay and Outwell in search of local 'talent' at their dances.

At the lower end of the town was the railway station. From there one could, if in the mood, get a direct – though never quick – train to London for a celebratory weekend. Just beyond the station the broad Great Ouse river flowed majestically down to the Wash, twelve miles further north. For those wanting to get away from it all this was a godsend, for the raised, green banks of the Great Ouse were about the only places where one could walk – apart from on the roads – without trespassing on valuable arable land.

But it was difficult to escape the war anywhere. Even when on the river banks, if walking towards Denver, one came eventually into contact with the military. At Denver Sluice, a mile and a half south of Downham, there was a guard at the end of the bridge and identity cards had to be shown to the sentry before crossing the river. The great sluice gates, constructed in 1825, kept the upper river at a constant level, thus protecting the low, flat, but agriculturally rich Fenland fields from inundation during high tides. The sluice gates were highly vulnerable to sabotage and, consequently, were guarded by the army on both sides of the river day and night.

In Downham Market itself, as if to emphasize the fact that there was a war on, all iron railings had been taken down in August 1942 and collected for scrap metal as part of a nation-wide salvage campaign. Railings everywhere, irrespective of whether they were ornamental or protective, private or public, were cut down from gardens, parks and schools and taken away to help the war effort.

There were other places to visit, either for a few hours or an occasional day off, further afield. Most personnel on the camp worked seven days a week and only had a thirty-six hours pass once in every three weeks. Usually the pass meant finishing work at midday and using the afternoon to have a shower, get tidied up and sort out clothes and kit; the following day was then completely free. For some Ely, with its towering cathedral, was the favourite place to visit. It was easy to get to on the train and was just about within reach by cycle.

**LAC Bill J. Overton, 218 Squadron**: There was a nice Salvation Army canteen in Ely where you could get a reasonable snack, and it was warm there. Warmth was always a consideration in winter when you were often cold and miserable.

Peterborough also had a fine cathedral as well as a good theatre, where the latest musical could be seen for a shilling (5p), but was a bit further away and more awkward to get to without a car.

The most popular venue was undoubtedly King's Lynn, a dozen miles to the north of the airfield. Being a port, with many historic buildings, it had its own delightful atmosphere as well as plenty of pubs, hotels, restaurants and a choice of cinemas. The Yacht Club, known to the airmen as the 'Ouse Booze', was a favourite spot for aircrews from both 608 and 635 Squadrons. The club backed on to the Great Ouse and was approached down a narrow alley which ended, a few yards past the entrance, in a series of steps down to the river. Restaurants varied in quality from the British Restaurant, where the price of a meal was a shilling, to the classy Duke's Head, which did a three-course meal for five shillings (25p).

**F/Lt Peter S. Hobbs, DFC, 608 Squadron**: We made occasional jaunts to King's Lynn, generally to the Duke's Head with its cockroaches, which you could race across the dining room tables between courses; or, perhaps, the Ouse Booze, provided one remembered which way to turn on leaving, otherwise one was liable to fall in the river!

But even the seemingly low prices were more than some could afford. For those earning only three shillings (15p) a day, with sixpence (2½p) deducted to send home, even the bus fare to places like King's Lynn had to be carefully considered before embarking on a day's outing.[7]

Because of its architecture King's Lynn had been chosen as the setting for a number of wartime films with Dutch locations. In earlier centuries the town had traded with the Netherlands and one of the results of this commercial interchange was a certain Dutch flavour in its architecture. With its lovely churches, medieval houses and two large, open market places King's Lynn could easily be mistaken for a town in Holland. The town scenes in *One of Our Aircraft is Missing* were filmed in King's Lynn in 1941. In September of the following year *The Silver Fleet*, a film about the Royal Navy, was shot in the town. Indeed, if anyone had visited the Saturday Market at that time, and had not been previously warned, they would surely have been shocked to find a German swastika flag flying from the fifteenth-century town hall, Nazi notices posted outside the building and SS guards walking around, while down at the Custom House there were 'German' sentries on duty.

For nights off duty the usual form of transport from the camp was the liberty bus. Those fortunate enough to own cars found that it was still possible to obtain petrol and drive to a pub or dance-hall. Aircrew were classified as on overseas duties and were therefore entitled to petrol coupons instead of rail warrants if they chose. Few civilians could get sufficient petrol to drive cars except in connection with essential business and so it was fairly easy to buy unwanted second-hand cars from local garages. It was also possible to get petrol on the black-market although one needed to be careful what one was buying as petrol was coloured according to its intended purpose to prevent illegal use. Thus Transport petrol was coloured red, aircraft petrol (100 octane) was green and pool petrol was yellow.

It was useful to have some civilian friends, as they sometimes had access to things not available to the airmen.

**S/Ldr G.M. Rothwell**: When we wished to go further afield for our evening activities we used to rely on a civilian who was attached to the squadron. He was an aero-engine representative and he had a car. On one occasion we had been to King's Lynn and on the way back we passed an entrance to a large country house. There were two stone pillars situated either side of the drive, each with a large round stone ball on top. We decided they would make excellent trophies for the garden of Bexwell Rectory which now served as the Officers' Mess. When we tried to lift one of these balls off its pedestal we found it extremely heavy but eventually managed to roll it to the door of the small Morris and by a superhuman effort get it on to the floor in the back. Surprisingly, it didn't go through the floor boards but it certainly slowed us down for the remainder of the journey.

Even with a car and petrol it was not always easy to get around at night during winter, what with blackout regulations and fogs. More than one story from those days concerns groups who had been celebrating in King's Lynn and then found it difficult to follow the road back to Downham Market. Sometimes a corner was missed, or taken too soon, with the result that both car and occupants found themselves in the Great Ouse. In one tale a car missed the road altogether on leaving King's Lynn and followed instead an unfenced single-track railway line out into the fields!

The vast majority of people living on the camp were, of course, male. There was therefore always an imbalance in the ratio of men to women. This, together with the fact that nearly all – whether married or not – were living far from home, naturally led to a desire to seek out local girls. Fortunately, as far as numbers are concerned at least, the local population had been supplemented by Voluntary Aid Detachment (VAD) nurses and girls of the Women's Land Army. The VAD nurses at Stow Bardolph Hall – which had been converted into a temporary hospital – were very popular with the men and often went to the Mess parties.

At Denver there was a Land Army hostel where a contingent of Yorkshire girls were encamped. This was another reason for the heavy use of the lane which led from the camp to Denver! Many of the aircrews were friendly with the Land Army girls while they, in turn, were adept at tuning in to radio transmissions from returning aircraft in order to find out who had gone missing on a raid. There was, however, a certain amount of jealousy amongst the women on the airfield for, according to one wireless operator, 'the WAAFs were not too happy if you were with Land Army girls at the cinema.'

But the local girls were not forgotten either. Airmen and local girls met in all kinds of ways. Most usually it was at dances, but it also happened that some girls were able to meet airmen at home when the airmen had been invited by their parents to come and relax while off duty. Sometimes the attachments became permanent and ended in marriage. But there were times when equally deep relationships were prematurely cut short by airmen going missing on operations. And the attachments were not only restricted to RAF personnel.

**S/Ldr Laurence E. Skan, 218 Squadron**: One American pilot used to fly into Downham Market regularly in a Lockheed Lightning fighter called 'Tangerine' (painted in large letters along the fuselage), park his aircraft alongside the Watch Office, report in to me, and then 'stooge' off to see his local girlfriend!

Many local families made their homes available to the airmen; some 'adopted' a complete aircrew.

**F/O B.J. Sherry, DFC**: We found that we were often invited home after closing time 'to meet the wife' and stay for a chat and a cocoa, in a real house in front of a real fire. These friendly folk were probably not aware just how much we appreciated being invited into the warmth and comfort of a home for an hour. We, in turn, would invite them along to a Mess party in an attempt to repay their hospitality. I have the warmest memories of these villagers.

Ron Bennett was one of the local farmers who kept open house for the airmen at Bridge Farm. The airmen were given complete freedom to arrive and leave just as they pleased. Often they turned up totally exhausted and used the farm simply as a rest place. In return some of the airmen used to help dig up the sugar-beet and earn a few extra bob as the season demanded. Many local people tried to do what they could for the men from the 'drome. It became a common thing to make friends with a local family and then to go regularly to their home for meals at weekends.

**Cpl H.W.S. Gable, Motor Transport**: I made friends with a tractor driver who worked on the camp, and his neighbour. They lived in two cottages at the end of a lane near the main road. The kindness they showed me I shall always remember, as they persuaded me to bring my wife and daughter from the coast just prior to D-Day.

At Christmas-time there were generous invitations to men and women who couldn't go home because they were stuck on the camp.

***LAC Bill J. Overton***: We were invited to spend Christmas with a King's Lynn family in 1943. After being stood down at midday on Christmas we cycled over to King's Lynn where we had a slap-up meal – even on war-time rations – and plenty of booze. The party fizzled out at midnight and then we cycled back to Downham in freezing fog. It was so cold, in fact, that the free-wheels of the service bikes froze up and and nothing happened however hard we pedalled until someone had the bright idea of unfreezing them by peeing on them!

Occasionally the locals came to the rescue when couples living on the camp needed somewhere to meet. Fraternization between the sexes and between officers and other ranks was officially frowned on and this made it impossible to meet openly and sometimes difficult to meet at all.

***Peggy Moorcroft (nee Sgt 'Tommy' Thompson), WAAF***: There was an old woman, around eighty, in the town called Mrs Bowman. She used to invite my fiancé (the squadron navigation officer) and me to her house and give us boiled eggs – a great luxury. Especially appreciated was having somewhere warm to meet, as fraternization between officers and other ranks was frowned upon. Many times I used to look enviously at lights in the houses between the camp and town and thought how lovely it would be to live in a house!

Leave for aircrew was six days every six weeks; if there were a number of crews missing then the leave might be more frequent! The leave was looked forward to eagerly and for most it meant, when eventually it came, a journey across unknown parts of Britain to home, wherever

*B Flight of 608 Squadron stand in front of one of their Mosquitos, May 1945.* G.A. Nunn

that was. Commonwealth airmen, who comprised a large proportion of aircrews in both 218 and 635 Squadrons, were, of course, not able to go home and therefore had to find other places to spend their precious and bravely-won leave. 635 Squadron was fortunate in that it had been 'adopted' by an Edinburgh business family and a large house, with all comforts, was made freely available in the Scottish capital for Dominion folk when on leave.

The journey home was usually by train, starting at Downham Market. There were those, however, who found other ways of travelling. Compass Adjuster Donald Eastwood, for example, managed to scrounge a lift from Downham to his home near Doncaster in a Halifax bomber which had been diverted. Peggy Moorcroft remembers hitching lifts on sugar-beet and potato lorries to her home in Essex. Perhaps the most curious way home, to Tangmere, was that taken by 218 Squadron's Flying Control Officer, Laurence Skan. The first part was easy: he just hitched a lift in a Short Stirling which happened to be conveniently going that way. Returning to Downham turned out to be slightly more awkward. He had been due to return by the same Stirling which had taken him, but unfortunately the plane developed a mechanical fault on its air test and the pilot decided to carry straight on and flew back without his passenger. Nothing daunted, Skan hopped on to an Avro Lancaster flying to RAF Wyton. He then continued his roundabout journey partly by train, partly in a coal lorry and partly in a petrol bowser. When, at last, he arrived back his Commanding Officer said: 'Why didn't you ring me from Wyton? I could have picked you up and flown you back.'

Leave was also used for celebrating and for this London might be, as often as not, the venue. The capital was easy to get to from Downham and while in London one could let one's hair down. Almost anything might happen there and probably did at some time or another. The exuberant, spontaneous spirit of those days is evoked by the following incident.

*S/Ldr Ian Ryall, 218 Squadron*: I was on leave with one of the girls from Stow Bardolph Hospital and we came out of one of those afternoon clubs of which there seemed to be many. This one was in one of the side streets off Shaftesbury Avenue. Outside the club was a chap winding a barrel-organ, playing a tune called 'Oh Johnny'. I asked him if I could play it and he was happy to let me. I then suggested pushing it down to the corner of Piccadilly. He obviously thought this a bit daring but, sporting chap that he was, agreed. It was quite amazing. A huge crowd, with many Yanks in it, gathered to see this Squadron Leader playing the barrel-organ while his girlfriend collected the money in his hat. People were singing and soon there was the beginning of a traffic jam. Several officers-of-the-law were trying to force their way through the crowd and we thought it time to leave. We tipped the contents of my hat (with quite a lot of money in it) into the man's collecting box and then got up on one of those brewer's drays which happened to be crawling along and were transported slowly away to the cheers of the crowd.

CHAPTER 4

# Take-Off

We have no graceful form, no flashing shape
To flicker, fish-like, in the dome of the sky;
No famous whine of motor, glint of light
Proclaims us to the earthling's ear or eye.
Darkly we go, unseen, by friends unsped,
Leaving the homely fields that are our own,
Up to the heights where sunset's early red
Changes to blackness. We are there alone.[8]

During 1942 a typical Main Force raid over Germany would comprise between two hundred and three hundred medium and heavy bombers from about thirty different squadrons. From mid-1943 onwards a typical raid was likely to involve more than five hundred heavy bombers. Often, of course, the raids were smaller but frequently over seven hundred aircraft participated and occasionally more than a thousand aircraft were sent to bomb a single target. It was highly important in order to achieve saturation over enemy territory, and therefore reduce aircraft losses, to get as many bombers over the target in the shortest possible time. To do this the aircraft of all the squadrons had to be carefully organized so that they took off at the correct times and arrived over the target, anywhere between 150 and 700 miles away, at the right moment. All this required precise planning.

Each day at nine o'clock in the morning the Commander-in-Chief held a conference in the operations room of Bomber Command Headquarters near High Wycombe. After hearing the latest weather forecast for the night, details of objectives in the area suitable for attack and information regarding the numbers of aircraft available, the C-in-C would choose the target and the H-hour, or the scheduled time over the target. Detailed planning was then begun by the operations staff and preliminary warnings were passed to each of the half dozen Bomber Groups. Each Group Headquarters then decided which of its squadrons should operate that night to fulfil the Group's part in the planned raid. If operations were not 'on' for the night or if Downham's squadrons were not needed the aircrews were stood down. The men then rushed to get their bikes and cars and dashed into Downham Market, King's Lynn, or wherever else took their fancy, and determined to enjoy themselves while they still had the time and opportunity.

But, more often than not, the raid was 'on' and the aircrews had to stand by in nervous anticipation. During the morning, details of the proposed raid were received over the red scrambler telephone in Downham's own operations room. For a few hours the ops' room, situated below Flying Control in the control tower, became the nerve centre of the airfield. The ops room had its own aura and superstitions, one of which foretold that if any aircrew put his gloves on the operations table then he would be for the 'chop' on the next operation! On the wall there was an operations board on which was chalked, as the information came in, details of the night's raid. The incoming 'gen' was noted down by a WAAF sergeant watchkeeper, who, owing to the shortage of staff, was sometimes called upon to work twenty-four hours at a stretch.

*Peggy Moorcroft (nee Sgt 'Tommy' Thompson), WAAF*: We would then be told that the night's operations were on, given the code name for the target and asked to provide a certain number of aircraft (from Downham). This information was immediately passed on to the station commander, the squadron commanders and the intelligence officer. From then on everything buzzed, and gradually, throughout the day, the rest of the information would be received. The squadron commanders rang back with their list of aircraft and pilots detailed for the night, which we passed on to all concerned. Group would then 'phone through the bomb load; which was always quite lengthy and complicated. All this was logged and the armament officer informed.[9]

Thereafter maps and briefing materials were arranged, navigation routes worked out, departure times decided and the fuel, ammunition and bombs loaded. Every day a meteorological balloon was sent up and automatically transmitted back by radio air pressure, wind speed and weather conditions. As soon as all details necessary for briefing had been finalized all contact with the outside world ceased and no outside 'phone calls were allowed apart from essential official calls.

Meanwhile, everything in each aircraft is gone over by the groundcrews and made ready for the night's operation. It is to the groundcrews and other maintenance staff that the aircrews owed their lives, as much as to their own tactics and good luck.

*F/Lt Peter S. Hobbs, DFC, 608 Squadron*: The groundcrews did a wonderful job under appalling conditions, spent long hours keeping the 'kites' in top condition, even more hours waiting for us to get away – and eventually to return – without the pleasures of seeing the pyrotechnics or the satisfaction of experiencing the final results of their efforts.

A groundcrew, usually comprising a sergeant, a corporal, four engine fitters and two airframe fitters, was allocated to each aircraft. Minor repairs, rectifications and last-minute jobs were

*Groundcrew work on a Stirling's Bristol Hercules engine in 1942. Imperial War Museum CH6312*

done on the spot, at the dispersal points, and for this work – done in the open, often in abysmal weather – there were no set working hours; only orders to get the work completed as quickly as possible! The fitters examined the engines, tested the magnetos, sniffed out oil leaks, inspected the airframes and checked the controls. They replaced worn parts, changed wheels and carried out any necessary repairs including those necessitated by flak damage from the previous raid.

*Cpl W. Pinnigar, 218 Squadron*: I was at Marham and came down in July 1942 with the advance maintenance party. Things were very primitive, although operational. We had a Nissen hut where we made patches in various sizes to cover – with a pair of 'lazy-tongs' and a pocketful of rivets – shrapnel holes in the wings. We cycled around the airfield asking if anyone had any holes that wanted mending.

Other trades worked differently in that they were grouped by flights and worked on any aircraft in the flight which required attention. Armourers cleaned and tested guns and gun-turrets and checked that bomb releases were working properly; wireless mechanics inspected and tested radios and transmitters; electricians checked a thousand and one things, including miles of complex wiring in each aircraft; instrument repairers adjusted the master compasses at the rear of each plane and the repeaters on the flight deck, and checked dozens of other delicate instruments and dials as well as the navigational equipment.

Much of the work was done by WAAFs, working far from home and in a male-dominated environment.

*Irene Forsdyke (nee Cpl Storer), WAAF*: A normal day (at Downham Market) began with our arrival at the Instrument Section where we read the barometer and noted down the reading. Next, we went to the flight sergeant in charge to see if he had any reports from the pilots of instruments having faulty readings, or other snags. These had to be dealt with first in case they turned out to be long jobs. For instance, if an oil pressure gauge had to be changed it could take most of the day. Our next job was the worst of all. We had to read the 'Board'. The Board contained a list of all the aircraft in alphabetical order, with those required for the coming night's operation indicated. On this board were one or two gaps sometimes, where an aircraft had been rubbed out, leaving a chalk smear. These were the ones which had not returned the previous night. We thought of the faces of the men who had flown in those aircraft, and had to pull ourselves together and get on with our work. Having read the Board we se' off to the aircraft with our tools, where we checked and set everything necessary.[10]

After the check-ups had been completed the pilot and his crew did a brief flying test to make sure that all was in perfect working order. The night flying test, as the test was called although it was carried out in broad daylight, might be just a few minutes' trip over to Wissington sugar factory and back, or a much longer flight, depending on the amount of work which had been done on the plane. When all and sundry had been checked and the aircrews were satisfied the men who were flying that night went back to their Nissen huts and tried, often unsuccessfully, to get some sleep.

While the aircrews slept the great four-engined bombers that stood at dispersals all around the perimeter of the airfield were refuelled, armed and bombed-up. The airfield had its own bomb stores, situated in woods as far as possible from the main camp. The bombs, mostly 4 lb incendiary (packed twenty-four to a container), 1,000 lb explosive, 2,000 lb sea-mines and 4,000 lb explosive, were stored between brick walls and covered with netting. From time to time the stores were replenished with bombs and ammunition brought by road from the main

*Bombs are prepared for loading aboard Stirling P-Peter of 218 Squadron.* Imperial War Museum D8974

stores at Barham, near Brandon, on the Norfolk–Suffolk border. On one occasion, according to LAC Herbert Crisp, 'a couple of 2,000 lb bombs rolled off a lorry near the church at Crimplesham on the way to the airfield'. Luckily, no harm was done. Mostly there was no problem with storing bombs except for the 30 lb oil-incendiaries which were unstable in hot weather and were kept near a water pit so that if any started smoking they could be thrown in. Once, in 1943, however, there was an enormous bang when some fused bombs which had been unloaded from aircraft after operations had been unexpectedly cancelled suddenly exploded. Fortunately, the bombs had been stored away from the rest of the ammunition and the explosion took place in the middle of the night; thus no one was hurt, but parts of a bomb-trailer were later found a mile away!

The bombs were carried around the airfield to the waiting aircraft in trains of low trailers pulled by tractors. Bombs less than 500 lb weight (used mostly for testing) could be man-handled into aircraft but all other types of bombs needed to be mechanically hoisted up between the yawning bomb-bay doors. The number of bombs and the amount of fuel to be carried were inversely related to each other and depended on the distance to the target and the flying conditions to be expected. In practice the aircraft rarely went in a straight line to the target but took a longer, more roundabout route, and this, consequently, affected the amount of fuel required and therefore the bomb-load. Thus, for a raid to Calais, 150 miles away as the crow flies, a four-engined bomber might carry a 12,000 lb bomb-load, but for Berlin, some 550 miles distant, it would need almost maximum fuel and therefore could only carry a 3,000 lb to 4,000 lb bomb-load.

As briefing time approached, in the mid or late afternoon, the crews gathered together in the briefing room near the Control Tower overlooking the main runway. After the arrival of the commanding officer a roll-call of all crew captains was taken and then a curtain on the end wall was pulled back to reveal a large map of north-western Europe marked with the night's target.

*Sea mines are loaded into the fuselage bomb bay of 218 Squadron's Stirling C-Charlie in 1943.* RAF Museum

The crews were briefed about routes to be taken to and from the target and were given information about bomb and fuel loads to be carried, take-off times, which runway to use and the recognition colours (known as 'colours of the day') for emergencies. The intelligence officer reported on the likely enemy opposition, either in the form of nightfighters or flak, and the met. officer (in 1942 still a civilian, but later a uniformed officer) reported on the anticipated weather conditions. The navigators and bomb-aimers had additional briefings so that they could organize the flight plans and bomb settings to be used.

The afternoon briefing over, the crews returned to their messes for a meal. The messes were in the lee of Bexwell church. Some called into the church where, in winter, a stove was lit every day to heat the ancient building and make it as welcoming as possible. LAC Herbert Crisp used to see to the stove fire, and noticed that many of the young crewmen used the church: 'Air-crew lads used to pray there before going out on "ops" and I often found coins in there for the Padre.'

The pre-flight meal for aircrew usually included bacon and real eggs. Real eggs, to the ground staff, who – like all civilians – had to manage on powdered eggs, were true luxury. After the meal the men changed into their flying clothes. The amount of clothes to be worn depended on the position occupied in the plane. The gun-turrets, particularly the lonely rear turret, were the coldest parts of the plane and in order to overcome the intense cold at night when flying high up above the clouds the gunners clad themselves in unwieldly, electrically heated overalls containing their own in-built Mae Wests. All the crew invariably wore flying boots lined with lamb's wool.

On their way to the final briefing or pick-up points the men collected their parachutes, escape kits and emergency 'iron rations'. Then began the ordeal of waiting. Would the 'op' be on or would it be scrubbed, only to be postponed for another night? A cancelled operation brought only temporary respite, delaying the inevitable, and the relief brought by a stand-down might be mercilessly reversed at a moment's notice when the 'op' was suddenly on again. Besides, a stand-down meant that most of the petrol had to be drained from the fuel tanks and the bombs and ammunition had to be laboriously unloaded from each aircraft, partly as a safety precaution and partly because on the next operation the crew would probably be going to a different destination requiring different loadings.

**Sgt Basil Brown, 635 Squadron**: On one occasion, there was a stand-down and all the groundcrews had rushed to the Downham pubs to celebrate. Then suddenly the 'op' was on again. When the men came back some were too drunk to do their work properly and, consequently, some of the armourers became careless in handling the bombs. A bomb was accidentally dropped (although not detonated) and one of the young erks became very frightened and went berserk.

Operations could become very erratic, for a variety of reasons. There was no guarantee that once alerted and ready that the night's operation would take place at all.

**F/Lt Peter S. Hobbs, DFC**: In two hundred days we completed fifty ops, at the normal rate of two nights on and one off. But the two nights on often meant four nights waiting as two of the 'ops' were scrubbed. One could be 'on' from eight in the evening until the early hours of the morning 'waiting for the weather to clear' before actually operating. This meant, in fact, a pretty relentless drain on one's resources; which though not, perhaps, felt while on the squadron, seemed to hit one once the adrenalin stopped.

The psychological strain on the airmen was immense. But the drive out to the waiting aircraft at their dispersal points and then waiting for the 'ops' to actually begin was, for many, the worst part about the whole business. It gave the men time to think and worry about the forthcoming ordeal and its likely outcome. This was the men's last chance for a fag or, if the take-off time had been put back, a cup of tea from the NAAFI van. It was always a period of tension and nervous uncertainty, made worse by the lurking possibility of last-minute changes.

More often than not operations were planned to start while there was still light. Usually this meant that planes took off during, or just before, twilight. For longer trips – to Berlin, Nuremberg or Turin, for instance – take-offs would be earlier than normal so that the aircraft would still be in darkness over enemy territory when returning from the raid. During the summer of 1944, on the other hand, when the allied forces invaded France, many raids were carried out in daylight. Occasionally planes left Downham very early in the morning, as on 4 October 1944, when 635 Squadron's Lancasters took off at 4.30 am for a raid on Bergen, in Norway.

Half reluctantly, half expectantly, the aircrew members climb up the metal ladder at the rear of the fuselage – or under the cockpit in the case of the Mosquitos – and make their respective ways to their flying positions. After carrying out last-minute checks the pilot starts up the powerful, 1,480 hp Rolls-Royce Merlin engines one by one, starting with the port inner engine. Each engine is warmed up in turn, gradually at first and then run up to more than 2,000 rpm to enable the superchargers, magnetos and constant speed units to be checked. The pilot throttles back and then speaks to each crew member over the intercom and they report back, each confirming his preparedness. With taxying and pre-take-off checks complete the pilot signals to the groundcrew to pull the wheel chocks away and then closes his window.

Slowly, in the lessening light, each heavily-laden plane begins to move out from its dispersal pad, using its outer engines for turning, and – like a herd of mammoth beasts beginning a trek – taxis along the perimeter track to line up at the leeward end of the runway. In 1942 there were rarely more than ten Stirlings available to go on each raid; in the following years there would often be fifteen, or even twenty, reverberating four-engined Lancaster bombers lined up darkly

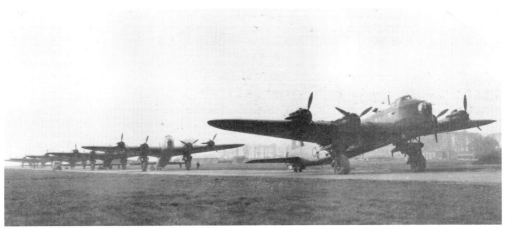

*Stirlings of 218 Squadron lined up on the perimeter track in 1942.* RAF Museum PO16027

at the end of the runway waiting for the signal to depart. From August 1944 there were twin-engined Mosquitos as well, but they tended to fly in packs of twelve to different targets and at different times.

At the end of the runway where the aircraft waited there was a caravan with the 'flarepath party', comprising a corporal and the aircraft control pilot (ACP). The caravan was connected by telephone to the control tower so that the ACP could phone the flying control officer to confirm when each plane took off. Others also gathered at the end of the runway to see the start of operations.

**Eleanor Zaleski (nee Cpl Bignall), WAAF**: I always put myself on night duty so that I could watch the boys take off. I left the Ops Block and went down to see them climb in to the huge Stirlings and take off. I know I had to hold my hat on tight! There was always a feeling of great excitement.

As the crews wait – some patiently, others impatiently – in their awkward and cramped quarters a green light flashes for the first aircraft to go. A final wave to the group of groundcrew and WAAF onlookers standing at the edge of the runway and then, after releasing the brakes, the pilot opens the throttles fully – the port throttles leading slightly to counteract the tendency to swing – and the great plane surges forward.

As the aircraft, carrying up to twelve tons of ammunition, bombs and fuel, gathers speed in the dusk the pilot moves the control column forward to lift the tail and, not far short of the runway's furthest end, gradually eases the monster off the ground at just over a hundred miles an hour. The plane races low above the ground, narrowly missing boundary hedges, strenuously trying to build up speed and height until it is safe to retract the undercarriage into the engine nacelles; then the wing flaps are raised and the dark shape begins its gentle climb into the twilight. As soon as the first plane has cleared the end of the runway the next plane turns into take-off position, straightens its tail-wheel and, after a pause to clear its engines, starts the mile-long sprint down the length of the runway and into the air.

**F/Sgt E.J. Insull, 218 Squadron**: Now it is our turn. The engines roared louder and louder and, with a 'hiss' of escaping air as the brakes were released, we started slowly to move forward – then faster and faster. We bumped and rocked but, when my Air Speed Indicator

*Stirling Q-Queenie of 218 Squadron runs up her engines before take-off.* Imperial War Museum CH6314

showed 115 miles per hour, the bumping stopped and I knew we were airborne. I made the first entry in my Log Sheet: '2240 hours – Airborne.' We climbed slowly in a wide circle. At 5,000 feet the Skipper told us to don our oxygen masks. With two minutes to go before 'Set Course' time, I called Tony and gave him the course. He began to turn slowly and passed over our airfield at 7,000 feet as he called, 'On course, zero six zero.' My next log entry reads: '2252 hours. Base, set course Cromer.' We were on our way to Hamburg, still climbing in gathering darkness.[11]

The night journey to the enemy target has begun. Each aircraft half disappears into the murky sky and circles around the base in a wide sweep, passing over quiet villages below – Crimplesham, Denver, Stow Bardolph – as it gradually gains height. Soon hundreds of bombers from all over eastern England will gather together in the darkness. There is no knowing what is in store for the airmen. For many there will be no return from the operation.

Some aircraft do not get to the target, do not even reach the North Sea. Some crews do not even get off the ground; not because of fear, although that was never far away: rather because of mechanical faults, faults which insist on appearing however well maintained the aircraft.

The Short Stirling, the bomber flown by 214, 218 and 623 Squadrons while stationed at Downham Market between July 1942 and February 1944, was, in many ways, a very good aeroplane which could take an enormous amount of punishment, but which, unfortunately, had two major defects. These were that it was unable to fly high enough to escape German flak and that it was notoriously difficult to handle when taking off and landing. Many Stirlings came to grief because of their pronounced tendency to swing when taking off. On one occasion the crew of P-Peter were very lucky when, according to Sgt Charles Weir, 'the plane swung off the runway and went across the grass in almost a full circle until we ended up behind the last plane in the queue waiting to take off.'

In the Squadron Operations Record Book there are numerous references to Stirlings that swung off the runway while attempting to become airborne. Sometimes when they swung the

*Lancaster U-Uncle of 635 Squadron at dispersal.* C. Godfrey

strain on the tall, gangly undercarriage was too great, causing it to snap and the plane to collapse in a crumpled heap. Once, in May 1943, a Stirling swung while taking off and careered across the grass until it ended up in the roof of the parachute locker room! On another occasion, in December 1943, L-Love tore through the pipelines of the fog dispersal system, FIDO.

> *F/Lt Murray Peden, DFC, 214 Squadron*: On take-off we were straining noisily down the runway at 90 miles per hour when, without warning, the aircraft cut uncontrollably to port. One second I was braced for lift-off; the next, we were bounding in a berserk charge across rough terrain. With throttles chopped, we tore dementedly right across the aerodrome, ran through a hedge, and finally fetched up on the far side of a shallow ditch. The Stirling was undamaged. Not so the great FIDO system paralleling the main runway. We had unhappily quit the runway through one of FIDO's main junctions, and taken an impressive footage with us.[12]

B-Beer was a Stirling of another kind – it never went on 'ops' on a Sunday! It carried out twenty-six sorties (ie, individual operations) altogether, but never, apparently, one on a Sunday. Always there was some reason why it could not go.

> *LAC Sydney M. Jones, 218 Squadron*: One Sunday, for instance, the plane was all bombed-up and ready to go and – as was the normal practice – the bomb-bay doors had been left open until ready to start, just in case there might be a stand-down. The flight engineer got into the plane just before the 'op' and put the switch on to disconnect the ground battery. Immediately there was a short-circuit and one of the bombs fell out onto the tarmac. As a result B-Beer didn't go on that 'op'. Sometimes, when an aircraft was unserviceable at the last moment, one crew would race another crew around the airfield to grab a spare plane so that they could complete their tour of thirty sorties as quickly as possible.

During the summer of 1942 the Stirlings also suffered from engine troubles. At the start of one operation in August a Stirling's engine caught fire soon after take-off. The fire spread rapidly to the starboard wing, causing the plane to crash in flames fifteen miles away, near Brandon. In the same month U-Uncle was forced to jettison its bombs over Gooderstone in order to lighten its load after an engine failed; luckily no damage was caused and the plane landed safely at Marham.

On 28 August another Stirling had engine trouble. This was T-Tommy, the last of seven planes that took off in the dusk, just before nine o'clock, bound for Saarbrucken. According to the Squadron Operations Record the 'port inner engine cut immediately after take-off. In order to save the lives of his crew the captain (Sergeant Elsom) decided to jettison his bombs and petrol while over Crimplesham. Unfortunately, some of the incendiaries caught fire although they had been dropped safe and in accordance with instructions received from base. The aircraft was then able to gain a little height and the pilot made an excellent landing on three engines. A very good show.'[13]

The incendiaries had landed in a shower around the Rectory Farm and within seconds the farmhouse and a nearby barn were ablaze. Two young girls, who had been in bed, had to rush downstairs in their nightdresses, while their elder brother tried to rescue a calf from the burning barn. There was a story, perhaps apocryphal, that the piano, which had been dragged out of the farmhouse onto the drive for safety, was smashed to pieces by the airfield fire-tender racing up the lane to help put out the fire. Fortunately, apart from a couple of pet rabbits – which were burnt to death by an incendiary – in the garden of a cottage close by, there were no casualties.

By March 1944 the Stirling squadrons had left Downham and had been replaced by a squadron of Lancasters. This was 635 Squadron and belonged to the famous 8 (Pathfinder) Group which consisted of squadrons specifically chosen to lead major air raids and to guide the rest of Bomber Command's forces accurately to the target. From now on Downham was in the van of the air-war. A few months later, in August 1944, 635 Squadron was joined by 608 Squadron equipped with fast, twin-engined Mosquitos. This latter squadron was part of 8 Group's Light Night Striking Force. The two squadrons of Lancasters and Mosquitos were formidable antagonists, but were, in fact, rarely used together in operations. Instead, they attacked quite separate targets and tended to set off at differing times.

Gradually, as the war wore on, the number of raids per month was stepped up until there was hardly a night in which operations did not take place. Sometimes there might be two, three, or even four, raids in a twenty-four hour period. Daylight raids became more frequent, although the majority of raids were still carried out under cover of darkness. The aircrews of both squadrons were, on the whole, very experienced veterans, being mostly on their second tours. In the case of 635 Squadron many of the crew members had been instructors in the Empire Flying School. In 608 Squadron most of the crew members had already done a tour of thirty sorties in Wellingtons or Lancasters. As weapons of war the Lancaster and the Mosquito were much more efficient than the heavy old Stirling and both were more economic in terms of men and materials. With the benefit of experienced crews and superior aircraft both 608 and 635 Squadrons were to become highly successful. Yet both squadrons had their share of difficulties, particularly at the start.

On 3 June 1944, one of 635 Squadron's Lancasters crashed into an airfield hangar near the Wimbotsham road immediately after taking off. All the crew were killed instantly. Three Australians in the crew were later buried in St Edmund's churchyard in Downham Market. F/Lt Ronald Wright was in the following Lancaster at take-off and saw the doomed plane take its erratic course before hitting the hangar.

*F/Lt Ronald Wright, DFC, DFM, 635 Squadron*: One very nasty incident happened one night during an operational take-off when the aircraft in front of us swung off the runway, became partly airborne, cleared the lane only to crash in farmland on the opposite side. The explosion which followed removed a farm building. The blast from the 4,000 lb 'cookie', target indicators, fuel and ammunition, followed by fire made the cause of the accident impossible to ascertain.

F/Sgt Paddy Cronin, also of 635 Squadron, had been off-duty that night, having a quiet pint in the pub: 'We were coming back from the Angel in Watlington and there was a big flash in front of us. We thought it was a German raid. The explosion blew out all the windows of a big house, where evacuees were staying, at Wimbotsham.'

Less disastrous, fortunately, was an occasion in September 1944 when 635 Squadron was lined up ready to carry out a daylight raid, in support of the army, over the battlefield area in France. Tubby Baker was Master Bomber for the operation, but as he took off one of his engines went dead. Without turning a hair he 'feathered' the duff engine and then set course with only three good engines and went on to take charge of the raid and complete his sortie.

The Mosquitos of 608 Squadron were, for all their exceptional qualities in the air, prone to problems when taking off or landing. Some accidents became legendary and, occasionally, had a humorous side, at least in the re-telling. In one incident, in October 1944, recorded by F/Lt Peter S. Hobbs, DFC, 'an Australian pilot lost an engine on take-off. He tried to gain height, but with a full load he failed to make it and pranged 150 yards from the Officers' Mess. The station medical officer, who was having a pint, rushes outside to see what was happening and then to assist. The Australian pilot says "Thanks, Doc", and standing in the cockpit grabs and downs the pint before climbing out of the aircraft.'

The crashed Mosquito was apparently not immediately assigned a guard, presumably because it was almost within the camp and therefore not considered to be at risk. Nevertheless, a few local boys managed to get close to the plane and took away the leg of the tail-wheel as a souvenir. Later, when they thought that the military police were searching for missing parts, the boys got scared and buried the piece of metal in a ditch where it probably still lies to this day.[14]

*Lancaster F-Freddie of 635 Squadron prepares for take-off. Note the automatic gun laying rear turret (AGLT).* Imperial War Museum BU5903

*Mosquito XVI, as used by 608 Squadron towards the end of the war.* Imperial War Museum CH5702

The following month another Mosquito lost its port engine while speeding down the runway at the start of an 'op'. As the pilot, Charles Lockyer, throttled back in a desperate attempt to avoid an accident the plane swerved off the runway and raced across the grass with its tail up. Unfortunately, a radar hut standing between the runway and the perimeter track lay in the way.

**_F/Lt Charles Lockyer, 608 Squadron_**: We duly 'collected' the hut and spread the Mosquito and the hut far and wide on the other side of the track, severing a cable in the process. Jock and I were knocked out cold, but he came round first and started to drag me out. We staggered out and, by a miracle, nothing blew. But we were both out of action for the next three weeks for facial cuts and some dental rebuilding.

According to the Mosquito's navigator, F/O B.J. Sherry, DFC, they were without front teeth for another few weeks and, when they went back on 'ops', spoke with pronounced lisps, but 'our friends gave us every sympathy and encouragement with remarks like: "You'll have to grit your gums and press on!"'

Added to the unforeseen difficulties of the journey ahead was the rule that strict radio silence had to be maintained by all aircraft during take-off and throughout the flight until returning to base. This caused its own problems as in the case of a Mosquito from 608 Squadron which developed engine trouble just after taking off on its way to raid Hannover in November 1944. The plane crashed a few miles away in the Fens. Because of the radio silence rule no one knew anything had gone wrong until it was noted that the plane had failed to return from the raid. The crew were posted as missing. Next morning the Mosquito was discovered upside down in a field near Friday Bridge. The pilot and the navigator were still alive but both very badly injured. It had been a bitterly cold night, however, and the effect of this, together with the injuries sustained, proved to be fatal for the pilot and he died soon after being found.

One operation which started off badly for 635 Squadron, but which, fortunately, ended successfully, took place on 25 March 1945 when F/Lt Alex Thorne, DFC, was Master Bomber for a raid on Osnabrück. When Thorne started up the engines of D-Dog the fuel gauges showed

*The crew of H-Harry of 218 Squadron in August 1943. The board shows the flying history of four Stirlings which carried the same identification letter.* E. Pierce, via John Reid

that the fuel tanks were almost empty. At first Thorne thought it was a faulty gauge, but then, having already started to taxi out on to the runway, he stopped the plane and had the tanks checked with a dip-stick. Sure enough, the tanks were virtually empty; there was only sufficient petrol in them for taking off. The crew jumped out of D-Dog and dashed across to the stand-by Lancaster only to find that its VHF radio wasn't working. They then raced back to D-Dog and managed to get a passing petrol bowser to fill it up. By the time the plane was ready to set off they were already thirty-seven minutes late and the main bomber force was almost halfway to the target.

D-Dog should, of course, have been leading the raid and so, to make up for lost time, Thorne was forced to fly direct from Downham to Osnabrück in a dangerous, straight line without the support of other aircraft. 'In the event,' Thorne recollects, 'we had no fighter opposition, but plenty of hostility from ground batteries. As we approached the target, the main bomber force came in behind us from the starboard side. Osnabrück reported extensive damage throughout the town, but no aircraft were lost from any of the squadrons taking part in the raid. The end result was, indeed, as planned. But it followed a rare, and probably unique, omission in the servicing of an operational aircraft.'[15] A few weeks later Alex Thorne was awarded the DSO to add to his DFC.

## CHAPTER 5

# Operations: Part One

No heat of battle warms our chilling blood;
No friendly soil beneath us if we fall;
Our only light the stars, whose fickle mood
Will lead them to desert us when we call.
Death down below or stealing through the dark
Awaits our coming with a silent grin.
Bellona's fireworks, curtained round our mark,
Form doors of fire through which we enter in.

The bombers circle around the airfield to gain height and then set course for the coast and the assembly point. At the invisible assembly point, high in the air above the coast, the various squadrons gather, alter course again, and join the stream of heavily-laden aircraft bound for the target. The assembly point varied according to conditions and the target chosen, but often the meeting place was Orford Ness, an easily identifiable strip of marshland lying between the River Alde and the sea near Aldeburgh.

From July 1942 to May 1945 there was a never-ending stream of aircraft flying from Downham to attack enemy targets all over Nazi-occupied Europe. In almost three years some 671 raids were launched from the airfield involving nearly six thousand individual aircraft sorties. There were periods, of course, when, because of adverse weather conditions, no operations could be carried out for a number of days together. But there were other occasions when there seemed to be almost constant activity at the airfield and two, three, or even four, raids were sent off in a single day. The objectives included land targets in Germany, Belgium, France, Italy and Norway and marine targets in the Bay of Biscay, near the Spanish coast, and in the Baltic and North Seas.

Operations or raids from Downham fall into two distinct phases. The first phase, from July 1942 to March 1944, covers operations flown by the three squadrons using Stirlings and is the subject of this chapter. The second phase, from March 1944 to May 1945, involving the two squadrons using Lancasters and Mosquitos is discussed in the next chapter.

On most raids the aircrew could expect to be in the air for anything from four to six hours with little but hope or anxiety, depending on each man's nature, to sustain them. On raids to Italy and the more distant parts of Germany the flying time was much longer and the men would be imprisoned in their flying metal cages for eight or more hours.

During an operation the crews had little chance to move around and were more or less confined to their respective positions in the plane. Of the Stirling's seven-man crew all, except the mid-upper gunner and the rear gunner, had stations in the heated forward part of the plane. Immediately in front of the wing section, on the port side, sat the wireless operator under the astrodome. The navigator's position, usually curtained off to prevent unwanted light seeping in, was just ahead of the wireless operator. The pilot sat under a glazed canopy on the port side of the cockpit near the front. On the starboard side of the cockpit was the flight engineer's station with all its panels of fuel gauges, switches, valves and control handles. In front of and below the cockpit was the nose gun-turret and an optically-flat glazed panel on the floor of the fuselage

*Stirling I, Q-Queenie, of 218 Squadron in flight.* Imperial War Museum CH6309

where the bomb-aimer lay in a prone position while over the target. A tunnel-like passage, festooned with miles of cables, pipes and ammunition tracks, led from the forward part of the fuselage to the exit and the unheated rear section. Halfway along the fuselage was the projecting mid-upper gun-turret where the gunner had to sit throughout the long journey with his feet dangling in the air. The rear gun-turret was situated at the tail-end of the fuselage, beyond the chemical lavatory and the master compass, and was only accessible by crawling through a narrow space between the tail-plane structural spars; it was the loneliest, coldest and least safe place on the plane. Crammed into the small rotating turret, without even room to wear his parachute, the rear-gunner was completely isolated from the rest of the crew; no wonder that he was referred to us the 'tail-end Charlie'!

During the summer months, when the nights were short, the bombers normally took off from Downham at, or just before, dusk, flew into the night while still over East Anglia and then re-entered the daylight zone as they climbed high above the North Sea. Usually daylight had faded into night again by the time that they reached the enemy coast. Nevertheless, there was often still enough light around to make this a dangerous time. The airfield's operational existence commenced during the summer of 1942 and the first couple of months was a disastrous time for 218 Squadron. Losses during this period, both from enemy action and from accidents, were exceptionally high. In September the nights began to close in noticeably earlier, despite the introduction of Double British Summer Time, and with cover of extra darkness the airfield's first squadron was able, at last, to draw breath and slowly its fortunes began to improve. The chance of any aircrew completing a tour of thirty operational sorties was still, nevertheless, frighteningly low. Gradually, as the war grinded on, the loss rate was brought down to a more acceptable level.

Stirling operations were mainly of two kinds. There were the Main Force raids and there were so-called minelaying or 'Gardening' operations. In the Main Force raids each Stirling squadron based at Downham Market was just one of many heavy-bomber squadrons operating from airfields all over eastern England which took part jointly in the nightly operations.

Typically, a dozen or more Stirlings would set out from Downham to join between two hundred and six hundred four-engined bombers from other airfields, all bound for the same target. Mostly the mainland targets between July 1942 and March 1944 were, either the industrial conglomerations of the Ruhr – 'Happy Valley' as it was euphemistically known – the port of Hamburg, or Berlin – 'the Big City'.

The raid carried out on 14 May 1943 was a fairly normal raid with sixteen Stirlings taking off from Downham just after midnight to join with 426 Halifaxes, Lancasters, Wellingtons and other Stirlings on their way to Bochum, in the Ruhr valley. For the crew of I-Item, however, it was their first mainland bombing raid, as the mid-upper gunner Len Durrant recalls.

*Sgt Len W. Durrant, 218 Squadron*: We were all very inexperienced and this almost led to our downfall. The flak was heavy and on our bombing run we were coned. The pilot did his best to free us from the searchlights. He was quite convinced that the safest place was underneath the flak which resulted in us losing considerable height and going around in circles. I am sure that we were still over Bochum when everyone else had left as there was no sign of activity except in our immediate vicinity. We had no knowledge of the extent of the damage our aircraft had sustained but we were aware that a piece of flak had clipped one of the prop' blades causing the aircraft to vibrate alarmingly. The pilot was loathe to 'feather' the engine as it provided the hydraulics for the turrets. We did eventually break away from Bochum and were very happy to see the North Sea.

When raids were carried out with small numbers of bombers they were often very costly in terms of airmen's lives. The raid of 17 December 1942 was typical of a small-scale raid in which very little seemed to go according to plan. A total of twenty-two aircraft set out to attack the Opel works in Fallersleben, but because of low cloud they had to bomb from heights of between 1,200 and 3,000 feet, well within range of the enemy's guns. The result was that only three aircraft managed to bomb the target through the cloud and eight aircraft failed to return. Of the ten Stirlings sent by 218 Squadron on this raid two were lost while the others were badly shot up. One of the Stirlings, in fact, returned with over seventy cannon holes in it!

Enemy guns were not the only way of wrecking our aircraft as G.M. Rothwell discovered to his horror one night in 1943. On 14 April sixteen Stirlings had taken off from Downham as part of a larger force and were on their way to the target at Stuttgart when, in the prosaic words of the Station Operations Record Book, 'E hit a pylon on the way out and returned early.' Apparently a new technique was being tried in an effort to confuse the German radar. All aircraft flew at 10,000 feet until reaching the enemy coast and then they split up. The Lancasters went up to 20,000 feet, the Halifaxes stayed at 10,000 feet while the Stirlings descended and flew just above ground level only climbing to bombing height when nearing the target. It was bright moonlight and whilst flying over Luxembourg the front gunner fired at various targets including a train and Rothwell watched the tracer hitting the engine.

*S/Ldr G.M. Rothwell, 218 Squadron*: When I shifted my gaze to the front I saw an electricity pylon dead ahead of us. Instinctively, I pulled hard back on the control column and the nose of the aircraft reared upwards – but too late. There was a tremendous crash and the whole aircraft shook and shuddered but continued climbing. There were vivid blue flashes coming from the transformer station beside the pylon. The bomb aimer reported that the incendiaries we were carrying had ignited in the bomb bays and we were on fire. I hurriedly opened the bomb doors and jettisoned the bombs whilst continuing to climb. Fortunately, the fire had not spread and the aircraft seemed to be behaving quite normally except for some vibration. On

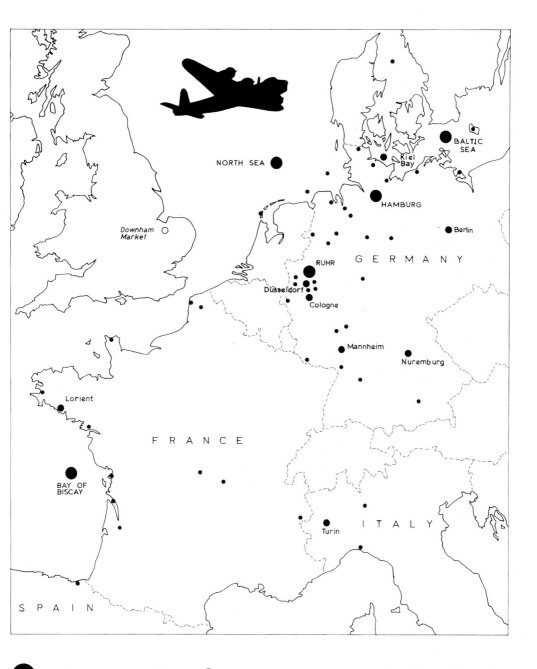

| ● | 100 or more sorties | ● | 50 to 99 sorties | • | 2 to 49 sorties |

*Location of targets attacked by Stirlings of 214, 218 and 623 Squadrons, July 1942 to February 1944. The main targets attacked (with number of sorties in brackets) were: mining, ie, Baltic Sea, Bay of Biscay, North Sea, etc (490), The Ruhr (196), Hamburg (121), Turin (74), Berlin (73), Lorient (68), Mannheim (67), Düsseldorf (64), Nuremberg (55) and Cologne (54). All other targets received fewer than 50 sorties.*

*Stirling E-Easy shows the damage caused to the underside of her fuselage after colliding with an electricity pylon over enemy territory on 14 April 1943. G.M. Rothwell, via John Reid*

the return journey we were attacked by two Junkers 88 nightfighters but the mid-upper gunner was able to drive them off. At our dispersal point after landing we inspected the damage and found the fuselage had been ripped open as though with a tin-opener from the bomb bay doors to the rear entrance.

Later the Ministry of Aircraft Production issued a leaflet recording the above event in order to extol the Stirling's unusual virtues.

218 Squadron participated in the memorable Battle of Hamburg and flew in each of the four raids carried out between 24 July and 2 August 1943, losing three Stirlings in the process. For the first raid the squadron sent twenty Stirlings. This was the raid in which 'Window' was used for the first time to confuse the German radar defence system. 'Window' consisted of bundles of silvered paper strips which when released into the air swamped the system with false echoes so that nothing could be distinguished on the radar screens. During the Hamburg raids the use of 'Window' proved to be so effective that initially it threw the enemy defence system into complete chaos and enabled the British raiders to bomb in such a concentrated way that a horrific firestorm was started. Attacks were planned to take place in six waves, each comprising more than a hundred aircraft. 218 Squadron bombed in the third wave against a spectacular background of green marker flares, bright flashes and widening circles of white light from the bombs, catherine-wheel bursts from shells and a seemingly aimless wavering of hundreds of ineffective searchlights.

**Sgt James McIlhinney, 218 Squadron**: It was a beautiful summer evening when we took off, and soon over the eastern counties of England, like a swarm of gnats, bombers circled and

---

# STIRLING BULLETIN No. 13.

## FLYING LOW IN MOONLIGHT, GOING TO STUTTGART, A STIRLING COLLIDED WITH AN ELECTRIC PYLON NEAR A BIG POWER STATION.

· BROKEN WIRES FILLED THE AIR WITH BLUE FLASHES AND THE STIRLING'S FUSELAGE WAS STABBED AND GASHED UNDERNEATH WITH HOLES. THE INCENDIARIES IN ITS BOMB-BAYS CAUGHT FIRE...

HASTILY THE PILOT JETTISONED HIS LOAD, SET COURSE FOR HOME AND MADE A SAFE RETURN.

THAT AIR-CREW WILL NOT FORGET WHAT THEY OWE TO THE BUILDERS OF THEIR STIRLING.

MINISTRY OF AIRCRAFT PRODUCTION.

Airframe: B.K. 650

| Engines: | Port outer: | SS 6202/A.308110 | Star. outer: | SS 6336/A.308244 |
|---|---|---|---|---|
| | „ inner: | SS 6424/A.308332 | „ inner: | SS 6268/A.308176 |

---

*A leaflet describing E-Easy's accident, issued by the Ministry of Aircraft Production.* G.M. Rothwell, via John Reid

climbed, setting course for the coast and the long haul across the North Sea to a turning point off the coast close to the Danish border. The short summer night drew in but we were aware of the vast concourse of aircraft heading northeast. Some distance from the coast, Window was dropped and continued as we crossed the German coast to a turning point where we turned south to the city of Hamburg. The task of pushing the bundles of aluminized strips down the flare chute was shared by the bomb-aimer and flight engineer, an unenviable job as they came back with blackened faces and hands, grumbling about the cold and discomfort of crouching at the back of the fuselage. As on other trips I climbed into the second pilot's seat but this time I was astounded at the different reception we received: searchlights were uncoordinated, moving aimlessly around the sky. We knew Hamburg was heavily defended but the searchlight batteries were completely confounded by Window, leaving individual searchlights to search blindly. Hamburg is a big city, but a large section of it was heavily hit; huge fires blazed, high explosive bombs burst like black mushrooms, something like shockwaves being visible around each. Our route out was between Bremerhaven and Cuxhaven... We were many miles at sea before we lost the fiery glow of Hamburg burning behind us.[16]

Of nearly eight hundred bombers sent to Hamburg only twelve failed to return that night; sadly one of these was that of 218 Squadron's commander, Wing Commander Don Saville (see page 88).

On the same raid J-Johnnie, the longest serving Stirling in the RAF at that time, was struck on the tail over Hamburg by an incendiary bomb from another plane flying above it. Fortunately, J-Johnnie somehow survived the accident and managed to fly back to Downham Market for the last time after completing a record sixty-one sorties.

The second Hamburg raid took place three days later on 27 July. Again nearly eight hundred aircraft took part for the loss of only seventeen aircraft. This was the night during which the catastrophic firestorm was started which eventually only subsided days later after all consumable material in the bombed part of the city had been burnt. For this raid 218 Squadron sent eighteen aircraft and all returned safely back to base.

For the third raid, on 29 July, twenty-one Stirlings took off from Downham just after ten o'clock at night. When the aircraft arrived over Hamburg the city was still burning and the crews could see smoke rising up in a mushroom-shaped cloud. Crews reported that the flak was moderate and searchlights were disorganized and that there was 'very thick smoke rising up to 10,000 feet'.[17] Altogether twenty-eight aircraft were lost on the raid, including two from 218 Squadron which were shot down over Hamburg.

By the fourth of the awesome Hamburg raids, on 2 August, the crews had started to get nervous and began to wonder how long their luck might hold out. The squadron commander's

*Smoke clouds billow up over Hamburg from the firestorm which had started two days previously. This photograph was taken by K-King of 218 Squadron from 16,000 feet on 29/30 July 1943.* Crown Copyright/MOD. Reproduced with the permission of the Controller of HMSO

plane had already been shot down on one of the previous raids and aircraft losses were beginning to mount again despite the use of 'Window'.

*P/O Reg Davey, 218 Squadron*: Our spirits sank even lower when we were again briefed for Hamburg. As we expected, the Germans were expecting us. We could not understand why HQ needed to wipe out Hamburg when we knew that there were far more valuable industrial targets. As predicted, we ran into a storm upon approaching the German coast and, apart from lightning playing on the propellers, we got iced up, could not see out and could not open the bomb doors. We blundered around until, at about 20,000 feet, our pilot, with help from the bomb-aimer, was able to work the controls and eventually we jettisoned our bombs on some lights we saw on the ground.

In fact, of the fifteen aircraft which had set out from Downham for Hamburg only three were able to bomb the target. Because of the severe weather conditions and the intense flak the rest of the planes either brought their bomb-loads back home or dropped them elsewhere over Germany.

The most distant targets were in northern Italy and entailed flying over the Alps, a situation for which the Stirling was not designed. 218 Squadron went to Italy on nine separate occasions. In November 1942 the squadron mounted three raids on the Fiat works in Turin. While generally successful these raids, like all the Italian forays, showed up the Stirling's main weakness – its inability to fly very high with a full load. One of the Stirlings sent to Turin had a maximum ceiling height of only 11,500 feet and, as most of the main Alpine peaks are over 12,000 feet, there wasn't much room for error!

*Sgt Lyndon O. Sims, DFC, 218 Squadron*: After stooging around a bit in the poor visibility, afraid of hitting a mountain hidden by clouds, we returned to base. The Commanding Officer was not pleased and we were sent back to Turin in another Stirling – fortunately a better one – within twenty-four hours.

'Gardening' was the ironically cosy term given to mine-laying operations. Although not without considerable dangers, mine-laying was a useful change from bombing mainland Germany. Mine-laying was also helpful for breaking in fresh crews and many a new pilot began operational flying with a 'gardening' exercise or two. There was usually little enemy opposition on the way to the objective but when the aircraft was over the target it was an entirely different story.

*Sgt Maxie Booth, 218 Squadron*: Ops to Kiel Harbour were worse than ground targets – not only had you the ground defences to cope with, but ships in the harbour also. We had four ops to the Kiel area – every one pretty rough.

Mine-laying trips were certainly no sinecures. In fact, it was on one of these operations, on 20 August 1942, that 218 Squadron endured its worst loss when *four* aircraft – out of nine dispatched – were lost and a fifth plane was forced to make a belly-landing at Marham.

On 4 November 1943 two of 218 Squadron's Stirlings were on mine-laying sorties over the waters of the Kattegat between Denmark and Sweden. The pilot of P-Peter was the squadron's commanding officer, Wing Commander W.G. Oldbury, who reported a fairly typical encounter with the enemy.

*W/Cdr W.G. Oldbury, OBE, DFC, 218 Squadron*: Our aircraft was flying at 10,000 feet . . . diving to break cloud to pin-point off the Danish coast. Rear Gunner saw an aircraft at

*Stirlings P-Peter and U-Uncle of 218 Squadron beat up the main runway at Downham Market in 1942.*
RAF Museum PO16028

800 yards starboard. The aircraft was climbing and Rear Gunner identified it as a (Junkers) Ju 88, gave orders to 'corkscrew starboard' and opened fire. The enemy aircraft broke away below to port without firing . . . [it] climbed and turned again from port quarter . . . Rear Gunner, Mid Upper Gunner and enemy aircraft all opened fire and enemy aircraft immediately broke away to starboard. It turned in from starboard quarter and Rear Gunner and Mid Upper Gunner opened fire. At this phase of the attack, during a 90 degrees bank all the guns in the rear turret stopped. [The] enemy aircraft attacked on three more occasions before cloud cover was reached, but our aircraft did a diving turn into it on each occasion, thus preventing the Ju 88 from getting his guns on and opening fire.[18]

The mine-laying trips were often very long – eight hours or more flying time – and were usually carried out singly or in very small groups. There was one occasion, on 17 October 1942, when only seven aircraft from the whole of Bomber Command carried out operations. All seven of those aircraft were Stirlings from 218 Squadron and, while the rest of the airfields in eastern England lay quiet, they departed from Downham Market to lay mines off the Danish island of Bornholm and the German island of Rugen in the Baltic Sea. Again, on 31 December 1943, while the rest of Bomber Command was preparing to welcome in the New Year, two Stirlings (one from 214 Squadron and the other from 218 Squadron) flew on their own from Downham Market to lay mines off the Dutch coast.

Not only were the mine-laying sorties boringly monotonous, but the crews also had the feeling of utter isolation – for each plane was on its own – and there could be no psychological

*'Happy landings – Q-Queenie': the crew of Stirling III EJ112 of 218 Squadron prior to take off for Berlin on 22 November 1943. This was the last Main Force raid to Germany in which Stirlings took part.*
M. Booth

comfort in seeing, or knowing, that other friendly aircraft were near. Much of the flying was at low level – sometimes only 500 feet above the waves all the way – and it was no fun trying to sneak up the Gironde estuary in full view through an ack-ack barrage or trying to slink across Kiel Harbour above the tops of the ships in a hail of flak. Before floating the ten-foot long cylindrical mines down to the sea by parachute the invisible dropping point had to be precisely pin-pointed. This sometimes necessitated flying over the water for a considerable time in order to locate the position accurately. At the end of it all there was no satisfactory explosion to be seen by the crew; only a tiny, silent splash – if one was lucky – in the vast blackness of the endless sea.

In November 1943 all Stirlings were withdrawn from Main Force operations over Germany. For the next three months, until the end of February 1944, 218 Squadron took part instead in mass diversionary exercises in the Baltic as well as carrying out normal Gardening duties. From time to time some of the Stirling crews also participated in air-sea rescue searches.

**S/Ldr G.M. Rothwell**: Later we took part in another search for nine Americans in a dinghy in the North Sea. We picked up an S.O.S. signal on the wireless and saw traces of fluorescence in the sea. Unfortunately the low cloud and sea mist prevented us actually sighting the dinghy but as a result of our message to base an air-sea rescue launch found the stranded airmen and picked them up.

# OPERATIONAL LOG BOOK

The following extracts from the Log Book of wireless operator Sergeant Maxie Booth, of 218 Squadron, illustrate part of a fairly typical tour of operations for Stirling aircrew at Downham Market. The notes in the 'Remarks' column are a little more descriptive than those usually found in Log Books and are helpful in re-creating something of the atmosphere and attitudes of that frenetic era.

| Date | Target | Remarks |
|------|--------|---------|
| *1943* | | |
| 2 Sep | FRISIAN ISLANDS | Mine-laying. Usual Flak, searchlights. |
| 3 Sep | LA ROCHELLE | Mine-laying. Usual Flak (heavy), searchlights. Quite uneventful trip. |
| 5 Sep | MANNHEIM | Very heavy Flak. Strong defences. Wizard prangs. Saw 2 aircraft go down. |
| 9 Sep | BOULOGNE | Very heavy Flak and searchlights. Someone baled out over target. |
| 15 Sep | MONTLUÇON | Little defences. Dunlop Rubber Factory well pranged. Could see fires 50 miles away. |
| 16 Sep | MODANE | Saw Alps for the first time. Bombed marshalling yards and railways. Defences very poor. Good prang. Starboard inner (engine) u/s over target – came back on 3 engines. Saw fires of Montluçon as we went on to Modane tonight. |
| 3 Oct | NORTH SEA | Air Sea Rescue between Dutch and Danish coast. No sighting. Search unsuccessful. |
| 4 Oct | FRANKFURT | Very heavy searchlights and Flak. Saw my first Gerry Night-fighter overhead, over target. One mass of fires. Successful prang. |
| 25 Oct | BALTIC SEA | Longish and quiet stooge. Iced up on return journey; fell 4,000 feet. Saw the lights of Sweden. Diverted by W/T to Lossiemouth. |
| 18 Nov | MANNHEIM | Very good trip but weather 30 (F) below freezing level. Searchlights and Flak as one duly expected. Good prang. |
| 19 Nov | LEVERKUSEN | Usual 'Happy Valley' expectations fulfilled. Defences strongest yet. Weather 25 (F) below freezing. Aircraft shot up; rear turret u/s. |
| 22 Nov | BERLIN | Turned back on reaching German border; icing very bad – 15 (F) below 0 ; wireless u/s. My biggest disappointment yet – not finishing trip. |
| *1944* | | |
| 5 Jan | LE TOUQUET & ABBEVILLE | Special Target (Flying Bomb site). Very little opposition. Good visibility. Good prang. |

| Date | Target | Remarks |
|---|---|---|
| 6 Jan | SAN SEBASTIAN | Flew at 1000 feet all trip. Very little opposition, but very, very tiring. Mines laid to order. Saw my first German convoy. Landed Predannock – Land's End. |
| 14 Jan | CHERBOURG | Special Target (Flying Bomb site). Little opposition. Uneventful trip. Excellent prang. |
| 29 Jan | KIEL HARBOUR | Mine-laying. Lived up to reputation. Weather pretty ropey. Heavy Flak and searchlights. |
| 12 Feb | FRISIAN ISLANDS | Very uneventful. Weather pretty ropey. |
| 15 Feb | KIEL HARBOUR | Mine-laying. 25 (F) below 0. All expectations duly filled. Very bad weather. In Lancaster stream on way to Big City. 218 Sqdn. aircraft shot down Ju88. |
| 17 Feb | NORTH SEA | Air Sea Rescue. Wreckage sighted. No dinghy seen. Search unsuccessful. Weather very ropey. Flew at 200 to 300 feet all trip. |
| 19 Feb | KIEL HARBOUR | Mine-laying. 25 (F) below 0. Heavy Flak & searchlights as per expectations. Went in Lancaster stream on way to Leipzig. |
| 21 Feb | FRISIAN ISLANDS | Low-level mine-laying. Lost one from 218 Sqdn. Apart from Flak & searchlights and ropey weather, trip quite uneventful. |
| 22 Feb | KIEL HARBOUR | Recalled by Group (due to weather) after crossing English coast 100 miles. Very cold. Icing bad. Returned on 3 engines. |

NB: 218 Squadron moved to Woolfox Lodge on 7 March 1944.

## CHAPTER 6

# Operations: Part Two

Flame, smoke and noise surround us for a while;
A shuddered jerk – the load goes screaming down;
Cold hands and feet move levers for escape;
A chain of fire bespatters through the town.
Back to the darkness, friendly now, we speed
To count our wounds and set a course for home,
Speaking to Base, attentive to our need,
Watching for that far friendly line of foam.

In March 1944 635 Squadron arrived at Downham. The squadron was part of the special Pathfinder Force set up by Air Commodore Don Bennett in 1942 with responsibility for leading major raids. On any raid there were different jobs for the Pathfinders to do and the individual squadrons which undertook these tasks varied from raid to raid. Firstly, there were the *Finders* who located the target area by dropping two lines of parachute flares. Then the *Illuminators* dropped flares to identify more precisely the actual aiming point. Finally, there were the *Backers-up* who dropped additional target indicator flares on the aiming point as the earlier ones burned out. It was on these target indicators that the Main Force aircraft bombed. Throughout a raid a Master Bomber from one of the Pathfinder squadrons flew around the target area while the raid was going on and gave radio instructions to crews on where to bomb and which indicators to observe or ignore.

Although Bomber Command aircrew were volunteers they were, nevertheless, normally required to complete a 'tour' of thirty operational sorties before being entitled to an extended rest. The rest period was usually spent as an instructor at a training unit. After the rest came a second tour – usually with a different squadron – of twenty operations. For aircrew serving with Pathfinder squadrons, however, the standard tour was increased to forty-five operational sorties in order to gain the maximum benefit from the men's experience in identifying targets. After forty-five ops were completed Pathfinder crewmen had a choice of either a six-month rest before embarking on another tour, or continuing flying, more or less without a break, for sixty ops.

*F/Sgt Wally H. Hitchcock, DFM, 635 Squadron*: In our case, after our first thirty ops, we had two weeks' holiday in Torquay at a hotel run by the RAF and then went straight back to Downham for another thirty ops.

635 Squadron's sphere of operations was confined almost entirely to Germany, Belgium and . northern France. The first four raids were all to targets over Germany. Despite the size and overwhelming intensity of these four raids – each involving more than seven hundred bombers – it was still considered safer to be at the beginning of the bomber stream (although then without the protection of 'Window') than to be further back. Consequently many aircrews did their best to get scheduled for the earliest positions.

*F/Sgt William D. Ogilvie, 635 Squadron*: We were only halfway up the bombing list and were Backer-Uppers, long after zero hour. We decided this was not good enough for us, so

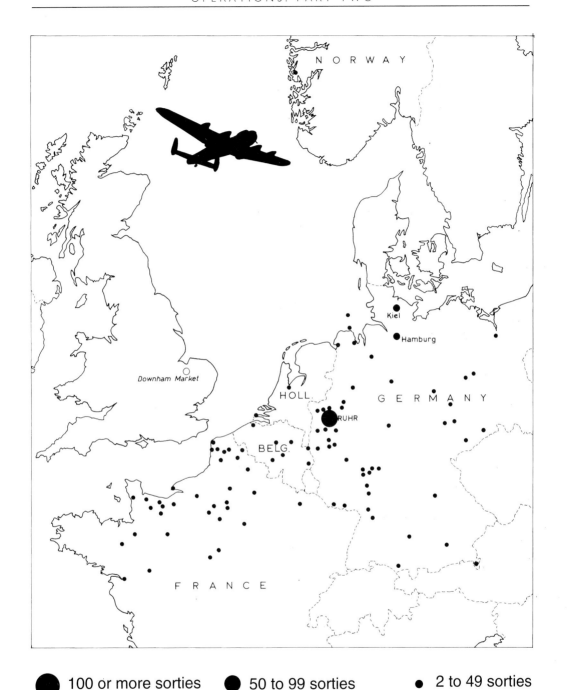

● **100 or more sorties**    ● **50 to 99 sorties**    • **2 to 49 sorties**

*Location of targets attacked by Lancasters of 635 Squadron, March 1944 to April 1945. The main targets attacked (with number of sorties in brackets) were: The Ruhr (352), Kiel (78) and Hamburg (73). All other targets received fewer than 50 sorties.*

we persuaded the navigator and bomb-aimer that we must get one 'aiming-point photo' to prove our worth. We did a very long, straight and level run into the target on that raid. It worked because we were back up at the top end of the list and were Blind Marker-Illuminator, at the head of the bomber stream (on the next raid) to Berlin.

But on the fourth raid – to Nuremberg on 30 March 1944 – this crew's zeal was of no avail, for although they remained Blind Marker-Illuminators their plane was brought down by enemy flak (see page 96).

The Nuremberg raid was the one in which Bomber Command suffered its greatest loss during the whole course of the war. Ninety-five aircraft were lost on this single operation – an appalling loss of just over one in seven aircraft taking part in the raid. It was also to be one of the worst nights for 635 Squadron; out of fourteen Lancasters which took off from Downham that evening three were shot down on their way to the target (see fig. 5). The cause of these losses was partly due to unpredicted weather changes and partly due to poor route planning by Bomber Command Headquarters. The combination of a cloudless, moonlit night, a sudden drop in temperature (giving rise to easily seen condensation trails) and a long, straight 200 mile flight across central Germany resulted in ideal conditions for the German defence system but disaster for the RAF.

The shooting down of another of 635 Squadron's Blind Marker-Illuminators during the same raid on Nuremberg has been recorded by a Messerschmitt Bf 110 pilot.

*Oberleutnant Helmut Schulte, II/NJG 5*: Normally our biggest problem was to find the bomber-stream, but on this night we had no trouble. I sighted a Lancaster and got underneath it and opened fire with my slanting weapon (*schräge Musik*, i.e. 'slanting Music').

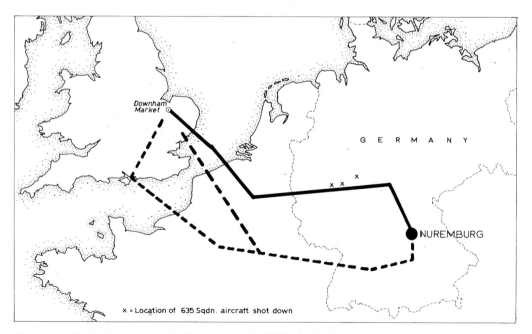

*The route taken by bombers for the Nuremberg raid, 30/31 March 1944. Note: the outward route is shown by a solid line; return routes are shown by broken lines.*

Unfortunately it jammed so that only a few shots put out of action the starboard-inner motor. The bomber dived violently and turned to the north, but because of good visibility, we were able to keep him in sight. I now attempted a second attack after he had settled on his course but because the Lancaster was now very slow, we always came out too far to the front. I tried the Slanting Music again and after another burst the bomber fell in flames. The crash showed that we had caught a Master of Ceremonies (i.e. a Blind Marker-Illuminator), for the resulting fireworks on the ground were red, green and white colours. I had never seen anything like it.[19]

Fortunately for the bomber crews the air battles were not always so one-sided. Occasionally the gunners scored hits against enemy aircraft despite being in slower and less manoeuvrable planes. Warrant Officer Bourassa was flying G-George towards Friedrichshafen on the German-Swiss border on 27 April 1944 when they met German fighters.

*W/O Bourassa, 635 Squadron*: Visibility was good with no cloud, the moon being dead astern and setting. Rear Gunner sighted (Junkers) Ju 88 dead astern at 200 yards. Order given to corkscrew and Rear Gunner opened fire. Enemy aircraft opened fire and tracer passed over port wing severing the aerial. Rear Gunner could see tracer ricochet off enemy aircraft. Enemy aircraft broke away to port with his starboard engine on fire. As Captain resumed course enemy aircraft was seen to be in a vertical dive and on fire. It was also seen to explode on the ground. Second Ju 88 was sighted silhouetted against first aircraft. Mid Upper Gunner opened with a short burst . . . enemy aircraft broke away and did not attack again.[20]

On returning from Friedrichshafen G-George was attacked again – this time by a single-engined Focke Wulf FW 190 – while over the English Channel, but after the Lancaster had corkscrewed a couple of times and its gunners had fired at the German fighter the enemy aircraft dived away and turned for home, much to the relief of the bomber's crew.

During much of April and May 635 Squadron's targets were switched to the enemy's transport system in France as a prelude to the D-Day Invasion and the opening of the long-awaited Second Front. On 18 April the squadron was called upon to supply a Master Bomber for the first time. From then on numerous raids were to be spearheaded by 635 Squadron.

On 5 June the squadron sent fourteen Lancasters to attack the German defences on the Normandy coast. At the briefing the crews had been told that the expected invasion of France was probably about to begin. 'When the crews returned that night, they were in a high state of excitement as a result of the amount of shipping they had seen converging on the Normandy beach-head. So dawned the much hoped for D-Day.'[21]

Although aircraft losses over France were never as bad as over German targets the raids could still be just as unnerving and distressing and it was often only by the merest chance that a plane and its crew came through it all. The story of K-King illustrates the point. K-King had taken off from Downham, along with seven other Lancasters, late at night on 11/12 June 1944 to attack Nantes railway station.

*S/Ldr H.M. Johnston, 635 Squadron*: We heard the Master Bomber instruct Main Force to come below cloud. When we came out of the cloud we had overshot the target so we made an orbit to starboard at 1500 feet. During the orbit a searchlight caught and held the aircraft and immediately we were fired on by a light flak battery, resulting in a fire breaking out in the rear turret and the elevator trimming tabs becoming jammed in a downward position. The ammunition in the tanks was exploding and I started to give the order to bale out when the intercom became u/s. We jettisoned our bombs. After much exertion I managed to get the control column back and the aircraft started to climb at an alarming angle to 2800 feet. The trimming tabs had then jammed in an upward position. I then repeated the order to bale out by making motions to the navigator and he, together with the bomb-aimer, engineer and mid-upper (gunner), got out. The rear-gunner had got burnt in trying to cope with the flames and his parachute was destroyed. The rear turret had fallen off by this time. In those circumstances I felt I had to try to keep going. The rear-gunner and the wireless operator continued their efforts to extinguish the fire and eventually succeeded. I was still finding it impossible to manipulate the control column, but by putting on varying degrees of flap I managed to get the aircraft straight and level although the airspeed was much reduced. The rear-gunner, although suffering severe pain from his burns, went into the mid-upper turret to keep a lookout for any enemy fighters. Meanwhile the wireless operator was sending out S.O.S. and getting fixes which he plotted on the navigator's chart and gave me the necessary alterations of course.[22]

All three of the crew that remained in the plane were given immediate awards for bravery: a DSO for F/Lt Johnston, a DFM for F/Sgt J. Ledgerwood (rear-gunner) and a DFC for P/O R.T. Padden (wireless operator) (see page 101 for the bomb-aimer and engineer's escapes).

For nearly four months after D-Day attacks continued to be made mainly on targets in northern France. Many of the French raids were made in daylight and included many attacks on German flying-bomb and rocket sites which then threatened London. Daylight bomber raids had, however, only been re-introduced with great reluctance for it was difficult to believe that the enemy would not be able to shoot down large numbers of our aircraft in conditions of clear visibility.

'When on June 22nd Wing Commander Voyce and Flight Lieutenant Beveridge took off as Master Bomber and Deputy to attack a rocket site at Siracourt in mid-afternoon we felt as if we were bidding farewell to a couple of heroes who were going out to tackle almost impossible

*A Lancaster of 635 Squadron, its bomb doors wide open, pictured on a daylight bombing raid over Calais, France, during September 1944.* C. Bowyer

odds. The tension was broken, however, when they returned from this attack and reported, "No flak, no fighters." This, unfortunately, did not always hold good for most of the subsequent daylight raids proved to be very costly.'[23]

Interspersed with the French raids were occasional longer trips to Germany, such as the one on 29 August 1944 to Stettin on the Baltic coast. On this raid thirteen Lancasters took off from Downham just after nine in the evening and made for the assembly point, 150 miles away in Durham, where they were joined by nearly four hundred more aircraft.

*T.J. Raymont, 635 Squadron*: Our usual D-Dog was not ready, so we had to take S-Sugar, a new kite which had only arrived a few days before and had not been serviced by our gen boys and instrument fitters. On take-off we headed north to Barnard Castle before turning east across the North Sea, keeping to around 500 feet for most of the crossing – hopefully to avoid German radar – and then climbing to cross Denmark and Sweden. This was quite an experience as the Swedes opened up with Bofors, searchlights and high flak; the orange balls of the Bofors guns coming up in strings and then curling over and going out well below us at about 10,000 or 12,000 feet, the searchlights waving about well to the north and the flak, high above and away from us, seemed to ensure our safe passage. I looked down and could see the lights of some of their towns – little groups of matchstick-sized twin rows of street lighting, such a contrast to our Blackout. Suddenly the navigator comes on the intercom: 'Hello Skipper, we are two minutes early; we need to lose time.' The Skipper replies: 'We can do an orbit or a dog-leg.' An orbit is decided upon and we start to turn to port. It seemed a long two minutes waiting to hear that we are back on course. Then, suddenly, whizz, I see two Lancasters pass about ten feet below us and almost side by side. I call: 'Get back on course quickly Skipper. We're crossing the main stream; I've just seen two Lancs pass below us at right angles!' It seemed that everyone stopped breathing, such was the silence, until a calm, clear voice comes over: 'Back on course.' We went on and bombed Stettin on time.[24]

From October 1944 to the end of the war 635 Squadron concentrated almost exclusively on German targets. Because it was part of the Pathfinder Group, and therefore responsible for guiding other squadrons on to the target, it was essential for 635 Squadron's own aircraft to be at the target on time. Thus the crews felt more pressure on them to do well than might otherwise have been the case and they sometimes went to extraordinary lengths to carry out their duties as effectively as possible. Even illness did not prevent some pilots from carrying on.

*F/Sgt Johnny P.G. Baines, 635 Squadron*: On one night operation our pilot was very ill and sick, but it was almost impossible to remove him from his seat as he was 6 ft 2 in and heavy. Not having a second pilot the flight engineer helped to keep the plane level. We found that some hydraulic fluid had leaked into the pilot's oxygen supply. He was given a fresh supply and he felt better and was able to carry on.

Unforeseen delays were boldly overcome by taking short cuts or by increasing speed, and thus sacrificing precious fuel, in order to save time.

*Sgt Pat Nolan, 635 Squadron*: The target was Kiel and we had a load of bombs and blind marker-illuminators. When we got to dispersal our aircraft was u/s and we waited for another one from the servicing hangar. By the time that it was bombed up all the squadron had already left and set course. The Squadron Commander came out and told us to forget our

ETA (Estimated Time of Arrival) and to go in with the Main Force, but the skipper decided to make up the time. We passed the leading squadrons of the Main Force over the North Sea at zero altitude. Coming up to the Danish coast we commenced to climb to 22,000 feet. But we were four minutes too early and so we dog-legged over the Canal to lose time.

Sometimes the best of intentions and calculations went wrong.

*F/Sgt Johnny P.G. Baines*: My first op from Downham Market was a daylight raid to Düsseldorf. There were very strong head winds. As we were Supporters for the Marker aircraft we had to be there dead on time, so we cut across country, but on arriving at the target the Main Force aircraft were nowhere in sight. We certainly took a hammering from the ground defences; also being a Supporter we had to go round again and over the target to drop our bombs on the second run in. We had about a hundred holes in the plane and I had a lump of shrapnel sticking right through the top of my rear turret, about two inches from my head. I still have the piece of shrapnel to this day.

Towards the end of the war seasoned pilots grew even more daring, or reckless, depending on which way one views it.

*W/Cdr A. Ashworth, DSO, DFC & Bar, AFC & Bar, 635 Squadron*: When I joined the squadron the Commander was Tubby Baker. We had the honour of being the supporter on Tubby's 100th sortie, which was to Wuppertal, just south of the Ruhr. We flew in formation to the target, which required a lot of concentration, as we had a full load of fuel and 18 x 500 lb bombs. I think the task appeared to be more difficult because Tubby and his engineer seemed to have a container of some sort in the cockpit and every now and then they raised tankards towards us with 'Good Health' gestures. The cloud base over the target was about 5,000 feet and Tubby dropped below this and called down the bomber Main Force. On the run into the target we were required to be about 1,000 feet below Tubby and some way in front. No bombs were to be dropped on our first run to obviate the possibility of obscuring the target with bomb debris. As Tubby attacked at some 3,000 feet it didn't leave a lot of room for margin and of course we had to drop our bombs on a second run. This was one of the most impressive demonstrations I saw on operations as the bombers came hurtling pell-mell down through the clouds, almost all with their wheels extended and flaps down so as to lose height rapidly.[25]

The other squadron sharing the airfield at Downham during this period of the war was 608 Squadron. The squadron had been reformed at RAF Downham Market in August with fast, twin engined Mosquitos. The Mosquitos were used for fast strikes at Berlin and other important German targets as well as for decoy raids. The squadron commenced operations on 5 August with just one Mosquito. The following night there were two Mosquitos, then three, and so on until the squadron was able to dispatch twelve aircraft regularly. The squadron seemed to be surprisingly little affected by the weather and operated almost every night until the end of the war.

*F/Lt Peter S. Hobbs, DFC, 608 Squadron*: As with most Pathfinder squadrons there were a goodly number of crews on their second tour of operations and they were rather taken aback to learn that, regardless of their previous experience, any first tour on Mossies comprises fifty operations!

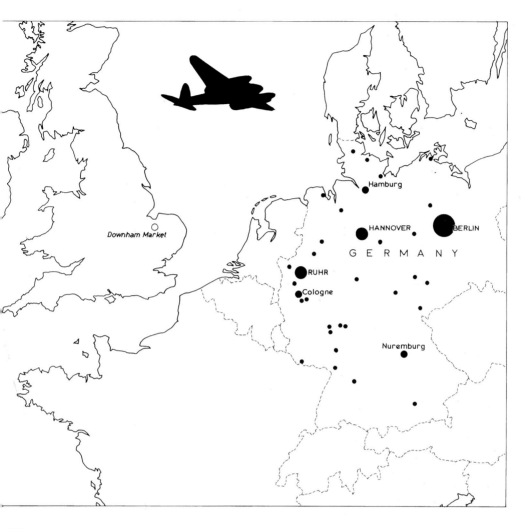

● 100 or more sorties     ● 50 to 99 sorties     • 2 to 49 sorties

*Location of targets attacked by Mosquitos of 608 Squadron, August 1944 to May 1945. The main targets attacked (with number of sorties shown in brackets) were: Berlin (726), Hannover (135), Hamburg (81), Nuremberg (57) and Cologne (56). All other targets received fewer than 50 sorties.*

The Mosquitos used by 608 Squadron were smaller and much faster than either the Lancasters or the Stirlings used by the other squadrons. Being mainly constructed of laminated plywood the Mosquito offered little resistance to flak or cannon when hit; the shells just went through one side and out of the other! The Mosquito's main drawback was lack of space in the cockpit which, when filled with so much technical equipment, left little room for its crew of two. Access into the cockpit was through a small hatch below the navigator's seat.

***F/Lt George A. Nunn, DFC, 608 Squadron****: The Mosquito was an incredibly good aeroplane, particularly the Mark XVI. I came back on one engine several times, after being

*A typical page from a 608 Squadron navigator's log book in March 1945, showing seven trips to Berlin in less than two weeks. H.S.T. Harris*

hit by shrapnel. But big people did find it a bit crowded, particularly the navigator. There was a proper pilot's seat, but the navigator sat slightly behind on a bench, and had to clamber down into the nose to do the bombing. He had a chest-type parachute, but the pilot had a lot of junk hanging on to him – he sat on his parachute, with the dinghy attached. It would have been hard for the pilot to get out if the navigator was dead.[26]

Fortunately, because of its greater speed, the time spent in a Mossie was usually a good deal less than in the other types of aircraft. A sortie to Berlin and back, for instance, would take just over four hours in a Mosquito, but seven to eight hours in a Lancaster or Stirling.

All of 608 Squadron's 232 raids were to the German mainland, the 'favourite' target being Berlin. Indeed, the 'Big City' was the target of no less than eighty-four raids. Despite the Mosquito's great speed Berlin was no easy target for it lay deep in the heart of Germany and was fiercely defended. During a raid the whole of the sky above the city would be lit up like a gigantic football stadium by thousands of searchlights; in addition, fast, single-engined fighters were sent up to hunt the un-armed bombers which stood out darkly silhouetted against the lightened sky.

The most vulnerable time for a Mosquito crew, and indeed for any other bomber crew, was during the bombing run when the aircraft had to be flown straight and level for a couple of minutes and both the pilot and navigator's attention were focused on the aiming point. After the bomb had been released it was still necessary to maintain an even course for another forty seconds or so in order to allow sufficient time for the plane's automatic camera to record the explosion at the bomb's point of impact. Then the pilot had to try to get out of the area as fast as possible.

While the raid is going on the enemy pilots remain vigilant and there is no chance to relax even when the bomb explosions have been photographed.

*F/O B.J. Sherry, DFC, 608 Squadron*: On our first trip to Berlin we had just completed our bombing run but as soon as I got back from the bomb-sight and started searching I saw a single-engined fighter outlined in the glare of the searchlights and only sixty feet above us. He had, fortunately, been vectored in by his groundcrew just a little too high and we were in his blind spot. It was a Focke Wulf 190 and its German Cross markings showed up clearly. He turned gently from side to side, hunting for us, obviously being told by his ground control that he was right on us and must be able to see us. We, in turn, synchronized to his moves, staying below him and in his blind spot. We continued like this for about six minutes – six very long minutes – until we reached the edge of the floodlit zone. He then turned back into the searchlight area while we turned in the opposite direction into the sheltering darkness and we started to breathe easily again.

The navigator of another 608 Squadron Mosquito, Harry Harris, remembered that they had just turned out of the bombing area and had settled on a course for home when, for no apparent reason, the searchlights suddenly went out.

*F/Lt Harry S.T. Harris, DFC, 608 Squadron*: I looked through the 'blister' to the rear of the aircraft and saw we were making extremely thick condensation trails. As I looked behind I saw a red and green light just above our contrail. I said to George, 'Some idiot is flying with his navigation lights on and is following behind us.' As I said this I realized the lights were gaining on us very fast. I then knew it was not one of ours but the dreaded German jet. At that moment a white light appeared between the red and green lights from the nose of the

*Mosquito XVIs of 608 Squadron in flight.* Imperial War Museum HU1634

aircraft. As it did I shouted, 'Dive to starboard – Go!' Simultaneously three things happened. The searchlights from the ground came on, bathing our aircraft in dazzling light. Secondly, George flung the Mosquito over to the right, pushing its nose down. And thirdly, a hail of coloured lights came across the top of the canopy. The fighter was firing and had just missed the cockpit, the cannon shells and tracer bullets missing us by inches. George said a rude word and pulled the aircraft over to the left. I was forcibly shot out of my seat, and crashed into the top of the perspex canopy. Then I was floating in the cockpit. Also floating was my parachute, which I grabbed and clipped on to my parachute harness. As I clipped on the parachute George said, very quietly, 'I can't see. I've been blinded by the searchlights. Bail out, quickly.' Having assured me that he would follow me out, I scrambled down to the nose, where the escape hatch was situated. I found the handle, but could not budge the door. Suddenly it was pitch black. The searchlight had gone out. I cursed then, as I could not see and I could not open the escape hatch. I gave it up and went back to George. He was still in his seat. As the aircraft turned over slowly, I saw fire through the top of the cockpit. I was looking down on the ground, and the fires were the result of the heavy bomber attack on Potsdam. I asked George if he could see. He had closed his eyes to try to get his vision back. As several minutes had passed since he was blinded, I asked him if he would open his eyes and look for the fires. Fortune was with us as he saw the red light of the fires, now on his left side.[27]

The plane had fallen about 25,000 feet and was now dangerously low at less than 2,000 feet above the ground. The cannon shells that had just missed the cockpit had gone through the rudder and tail fin instead. Carefully the pilot, F/Lt George Nunn, DFC, brought the plane on to an even keel and then, gradually, began to gain height. The instruments had gone berserk and, for a while, most were useless. 'I flew back on the Turn and Bank Indicator until the instruments recovered. We were minus half the tail, but this didn't affect the flying qualities of the aircraft.'[28]

*F/Lt Harry S.T. Harris, DFC, and F/Lt George A. Nunn, DFC, in front of their Mosquito XXV. Note the long-range fuel tanks under the wings. G.A. Nunn*

When not raiding Berlin 608 Squadron would, as often as not, join in with the heavy bombers, but not necessarily to bomb the same targets.

***W/Cdr Peter McDermott, DFC, DFM, 608 Squadron***: We also flew decoy raids, taking off after the Main Force of Lancasters and Halifaxes, flying through it (– not to be recommended on dark nights to the faint-hearted), beginning to drop 'Window' as we emerged from the head of the Main Force and then turning off, hoping to draw the German nightfighters after us and so leaving the Main Force unmolested. Other jobs were patrolling over the target and dropping anti-flak and anti-fighter 'Window' to provide some protection for the Main Force; this gave one a grandstand view of the development of the raid for some twenty minutes or so.

'Window' was released through a raked chute in the floor just ahead of the navigator. The chute had a spring flap and the navigator was forced to puff and pant in the rarefied air while he pushed bundles of 'Window' out as quickly as possible. Once through the chute the slipstream of the plane created a powerful suction that tended to attract any loose material nearby. This could sometimes cause problems, as in the case of the navigator who lost part of his chart.

***F/Lt Cecil Jacobs, DFC, 608 Squadron***: Unfortunately, as he (the navigator) bent down to push out the bundles the Gee Chart slipped off his lap and was almost sucked out with the 'Window' down the chute. He caught the end of it and was left with a jagged edge in his hand. It was the bit with England on it, so after the target we just steered a 280 degree course until we came back onto the chart a few miles off the coast of East Anglia.

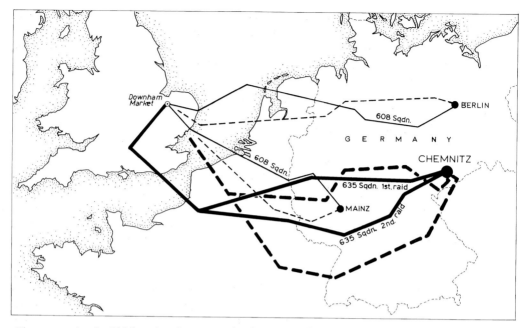

*The routes taken by 635 Squadron Lancasters for the main raids to Chemnitz and for diversionary raids by 608 Squadron Mosquitos to Berlin and Mainz on 14/15 February 1945. Note: the outward routes are shown by solid lines; return routes are shown by broken lines.*

Combined operations were often extremely complicated and involved much elaborate planning beforehand. One such operation, known as 'Thunderclap', took place on 14 February 1945 and included a Main Force assault on Chemnitz in eastern Germany, a smaller force attack on the Rositz oil refinery and diversionary forays to the North Sea and the Baltic Sea and raids to Berlin, Dessau, Duisburg, Frankfurt and Mainz.

For this operation each of the Downham Market squadrons was split into two sections. The first ten Lancasters of 635 Squadron took off just before half-past five in the afternoon and followed a circuitous route across France and Belgium to join the Main Force over Chemnitz. An hour later six Mosquitos of 608 Squadron left for a 'spoof' raid on Mainz and at seven o'clock a further six Mosquitos took off bound for Berlin. The main raid on Chemnitz commenced at 8.15 pm and four minutes later the raid began on Berlin. The second phase of the main raid on Chemnitz began three hours later and included a further six Lancasters from 635 Squadron. Only one aircraft was lost from the twenty-eight which had taken part from Downham. It was, nevertheless, a disappointing operation for despite all the careful organization there was thick cloud over the target and most of the bombs fell harmlessly in open countryside.

The usual bombing height for the Mosquitos was about 25,000 feet, although sometimes it could be even higher. Oxygen was vital when flying at these high altitudes, and normally a crew switched on the oxygen while taxying out before take-off and kept the supply on throughout the trip. A fractured, or badly connected oxygen pipe could be as lethal as anything the enemy could do and probably many aircrew were lost as a result of flak damage to their oxygen supply lines.

After the German break-through in December 1944 during the Ardennes counter-offensive 608 Squadron was switched to low-level attacks on railway targets and, in particular, the enemy supply routes. These targets were usually attacked at about 4,000 feet, the minimum safe height when carrying 4,000 lb bombs. At this height the Mosquitos were very exposed to flak, but although many of the planes were hit few were brought down and the Mossie retained its enviable record of always (or, at least, nearly always) getting through.

608 Squadron also flew a small number of high-level daylight raids during the last few months of the war. These were, if anything, less welcome to the crews.

*F/O B.J. Sherry, DFC*: After a long spell night bombing, it was an unusual and unnerving feeling venturing out over Germany in broad daylight, particularly the Ruhr. We set off from Downham for Duisburg in formation and picked our Oboe Markers at our appointed position over the North Sea, but there was no sign of our fighter escort at the rendezvous. We pushed on feeling naked and very vulnerable in a bright blue, almost cloudless sky streaked with contrails which you could see for miles. At least the promised cloud sheet was covering the land. After about fifteen minutes flying into Germany we suddenly spotted a formation of fighters with squared off wing tips high above us . . . American Mustangs or German Focke Wulf 190s? They started to come down to our level and, to our relief, turned out to be Mustangs. We were now north of the target and turned on to our last leg, the long bombing run down to the release point. After a few initial, minor adjustments the Oboe Markers settled down to a rock-steady course. The pilots were fully occupied, flying a tight formation in twin lines behind the Markers. The navigators, with not enough to do, were keeping an eye open for enemy fighters and wondering when the flak was going to arrive. I remember taking my mind off things by working out an emergency course that would take us to the nearest allied-occupied territory in the event of being hit. The Oboe Markers opened their bomb-doors and everyone else followed suit. Then the flak arrived. With the first bursts, the fighter escort scattered in all directions. One minute they were there, close by, then the next, they were far out on both flanks where they continued to eye us with a morbid interest from afar. We continued to plough on through the flak, flying through bursts of smoke, straight and level, locked on an invisible, electronic guideline leading to the release point. Fortunately, no one was forced to drop out and, after what seemed like an eternity, the release point was reached, the Markers cleared their bomb-bays and everyone else bombed on salvo. With that the formation loosened up, turned away from the target and headed for home. Shortly afterwards the flak stopped.

CHAPTER 7

# Return and Landfall

Hour upon hour the long-drawn journey runs;
Fighters and searchlights still our road proclaim.
Salt-eyed, we watch the heavens for the Huns,
Weary, we dodge the heaven-splitting flame.
Then, with no certain vict'ry to impart,
Out of the dawn we drop from frosty height,
Welcomed alone by those who saw us start
And watched and waited for us through the night.

Until the time when the bombers arrive back over Britain, and are nearing the airfield, strict radio silence was maintained except for dire emergencies. For hours the VHF radio – switched on for listening-in to only – has been silent, apart from an occasional laconic message.

*F/O B.J. Sherry, DFC, 608 Squadron*: I remember one particular night coming back over northern Germany at 36,000 feet . . . dense cloud below, clear sky above and stars brilliant. It was very cold and well below freezing in the cabin. Rime was forming on the inside of my observation blister and I was scraping it off with my plastic Douglas protractor, when the time came to change the wavelength on the VHF radio. Chas pressed the button and the cabin was flooded with sound; it was music from the Swan Lake ballet and was coming from somewhere close by in Germany. We flew on for about twenty minutes with the sound of Swan Lake slowly fading as we distanced ourselves from the transmitter. It's interesting how something quite irrelevant, like a scent or a melody, happening at the time gets tied into the memory and forever after acts as a key to unlock that time and place. The beginning of Swan Lake does that for me. Any time I hear it I am immediately back: high up in the cold and dark under the stars, with the muffled roar of aero-engines and that glorious music flooding the cabin – heading for home.

Then, as the planes near home, the air-waves become alive with calls from wireless operators radioing in for instructions or for help. 'Hello, Off-strike, this is Q-Queenie calling. What is my turn to land?', and so on.

Gradually, as the chatter of radio traffic between the bombers and the East Anglian airfields builds up, the air becomes filled with the sound of girls' voices. The 'girls' are the WAAF ground-radio operators whose sonorous voices come across clearly through the static and interference where many a man's deeper sound would have been indistinguishable and lost. For the weary crews returning from their hazardous bombing missions the voices of the WAAF radio operators must often have seemed like the sounds of angels. Just hearing their friendly voices was a psychological boost to the tired and stressed returning airmen.

*F/O B.J. Sherry, DFC*: One started to recognize certain voices and call-signs, to wonder what she looked like . . . what she would be like to talk to without the clipped jargon of R/T procedure. But it was dangerous to relax and day-dream before you were back on the ground. We were sometimes followed in by intruders and could be shot up in the act of landing.

But it was not only the WAAF girls who stayed up listening for the returning bombers. Anyone who was patient enough to spend a bit of time fiddling around with the radio tuner could pick up the transmissions between the incoming planes and Flying Control. My father used to listen in on his radio, just as many others did and as, too, did the girls of the Women's Land Army living at Denver hostel.

*Sgt Maxie Booth, 218 Squadron*: There was a contingent of Land Army girls from Yorkshire there at the time. These girls knew a lot about our flying. They told us that they listened in to the wireless early each morning when our R/T equipment could be picked up and they used to know exactly which aircraft had got back safely.

The journey back from the target to Downham was frequently long and perilous and was always fraught with tension. Sometimes it was too easy to start feeling that the problems of the night were over; but that way lay danger. It was on the return journey, when crews were tired, that the enemy fighters often attacked with most success. Again, there was always an element of luck as to which plane was hit and which wasn't, but the crews that kept vigil without relaxing and the pilots that continued to change height regularly and maintain a weaving course had a better chance of returning than those that did not.

*S/Ldr Ian Ryall, 218 Squadron*: One trip I remember particularly. That was the Peenemünde one.[29] The trip out was easy. The Germans had thought, as they were meant to think, that we were going to Berlin, but by the time we were going home they had got themselves organized and the fun started as we were flying over Denmark. It was bright moonlight, clear and very still – the sort of night when one felt the sheer pleasure of flying and it was difficult not to relax and forget the war. Then it started. One of the gunners reported tracer fire out to one side; then there was a glow in the sky rapidly becoming brighter and starting to spiral down. This was going on all around us; some aircraft blowing up in the air, some when they hit the ground. We were lucky. Or perhaps it wasn't all luck. We never flew at the same height or on the same course for more than a minute or so, keeping up a continuous weave. Maybe we were a bit harder to find than some others.

Fuel, or rather the lack of it, was one of the perennial problems associated with deep penetration raids. Any deviation from the planned route, either as a result of strong winds, poor navigation or harassment by enemy fighters, might mean that the plane could run short of fuel before arriving home. In addition, a very cautious engineer might change over from one fuel tank to another before absolutely necessary thus leaving a few precious gallons of unused petrol in each tank. Stirlings had fourteen separate tanks – seven in each wing – and they were especially vulnerable to this possibility; a returning Stirling could easily end up with nearly a hundred gallons of unusable petrol, enough for half an hour's flying. The Lancaster, on the other hand, had only six tanks to carry almost as much fuel and hence the problem of unusable fuel was not so acute.

It is worth re-telling the story of how the Stirling's notorious thirst for fuel was put to good use on one occasion in December 1942. The Stirling in question had left Downham to bomb Mannheim. The journey to the target had been pretty rough and then, on the return, the crew somehow lost their way. Suddenly the coast appeared but no one had any idea which part of the coast it was or how far they were from base. The flight engineer, realizing that they were lost, craftily, and deliberately misleadingly, reported that they were running short of fuel. The pilot, knowing how unpredictable the plane was for fuel consumption, persuaded the wireless

*Stirling S-Sugar of 218 Squadron at dispersal in 1942. Note two more Stirlings in the background, partly hidden on their wooded dispersal pads.* RAF Museum PO16029

operator to send an S.O.S. signal for help. The radio signal was picked up and 'sandra lights' were switched on to form a distinctive cone of light beams over the Sussex coast, thus indicating the way to England and, in particular, to RAF Tangmere where the Stirling eventually landed.

The Mosquitos of 608 Squadron had a somewhat different fuel problem.

*F/O B.J. Sherry, DFC*: For long trips, like Berlin, we carried extra fuel in drop tanks slung under the wings. The usual routine was to use the petrol in the plane's outer wing tanks first and, once there was room, the petrol from the drop tanks was siphoned over into the 'outers'. It was always a bit of a relief when this was accomplished successfully. Sometimes, because of the altitude, the transfer would not take place due to an air-lock developing, and you were stuck carrying 120 gallons of fuel in the empty tanks that you couldn't get at. These air-locks usually resolved themselves when you descended to a lower altitude, but you could be half way back across the North Sea and beginning to run short of fuel before you knew whether this was going to happen or not. Occasionally both 608 Squadron and 635 Squadron would arrive back at Downham from their respective operations at the same time. In these circumstances 608 Squadron would be given priority in landing because of the greater urgency of their fuel problems.

With fuel low and maybe damage to some part of the airplane the return journey across the North Sea was often fraught with tension. It was too soon to relax for there were still ample opportunities for disaster and a dive into the 'drink' certainly did not enhance one's chances of survival.

*P/O Reg Davey, 218 Squadron*: I shall never forget the enormous relief at crossing our coast on return, just as dawn was breaking. The ground was first coloured a misty mauve which changed to dark green and then light green. Once we were over East Anglia there was always a race to join the circuit and get an early turn for landing, otherwise it could mean a considerable wait for de-briefing as there were usually only three intelligence officers on duty.

The airfield at Downham was relatively easy to locate from amongst all the other airfields in the area; it lay mid-way between a lake at Stradsett and a distinctive junction of two rigidly straight rivers, the Old Bedford and the New Bedford. From the air, these physical features were unmistakable and, in moonlight, reflected clearly.

When each returning plane came within radio-transmission range the pilot called Flying Control with the station call-sign and, after identifying his aircraft, asked for permission to land. The control officer himself, or one of the WAAF radio operators, replied giving directions for landing or, alternatively, instructions to fly in circuit at a prescribed height. If a number of aircraft returned at approximately the same time they were 'stacked' vertically 500 feet apart as they joined the circuit. As each aircraft landed the others were stepped down to the next lower height band until it became their turn to land. At the same time discs, each with a letter on it representing an aircraft, were moved on a board in the Control Room to follow the aircraft movements so that the control officer could read the overall situation at any time. When each aircraft landed its time of landing was chalked up on the blackboard. Too often, however, time went by and still one of the planes had not called in. It was then that the long, sad wait began until it was clear beyond any doubt that its fuel had run out and then the word MISSING was chalked up on the board.

In theory the landing procedure was supposed to work smoothly. At Downham a speedy landing system was developed so that as one aircraft was turning off the runway the next one was touching down and a third was just turning in off the circuit.

*S/Ldr Laurence E. Skan, Flying Control Officer, 218 Squadron*: Inevitably smoothness was interrupted if an aircraft called that it was short of petrol and must land immediately, or was shot-up or had injured on board. That aircraft was then given priority as soon as the runway was clear. So far as damaged aircraft were concerned, care had to be exercised in giving priority as, of course, it could mean a blocked runway. Despite all the care, sometimes an aircraft would crash on landing and, before deciding whether diversion to another airfield was essential, the control officer would dash out in a car or van to see whether the crash was sufficiently clear of the runway to make it reasonably safe to land the remaining aircraft.

The returning aircraft land one by one while the people in the surrounding villages still lie asleep in their warm beds. As each aircraft landed the time was chalked up on the blackboard. Those airmen fortunate enough to have survived uninjured are more than grateful to be back.

*S/Ldr Ian Ryall*: You return to base and pull off a smooth landing. Someone in the crew makes a joke about it and you are pleased. Then in to de-briefing where, over a steaming mug of coffee laced with rum, you go over the whole trip again for the record. Then back to the Mess and bacon and eggs. If the worst has happened, and one of your friends has failed to get back, you may, by prior agreement, have his eggs as well as your own. And so to bed.

Bombing Germany was dangerous and exhausting work and the faces of the returning airmen showed the strain and effort. Mrs Pointer was a WAAF in the signals section at the airfield and remembers seeing the men when they returned from operations.

I recall how they used to report back from operations looking as if they had been sweeping the chimney, their faces covered in oil and soot. The first time I saw a crew in this state I just couldn't believe it. I particularly recall one Engineer who would come in and bring the remainder of his chocolate and fruit and nut ration to the girls on duty, no doubt again tied up with superstition.[30]

*A 218 Squadron crew at de-briefing after returning from a raid. Watching the proceedings are members of the Brazilian Mission who visited Downham Market, November 1943.* Imperial War Museum CH11650

When the aircraft were safely down and back at their dispersal points then the groundcrews got busy, inspecting their charges for any battle-damage or other faults and generally making sure that they were ready for the next operation. Minor repairs had to be made to any flak damage. The groundcrews of the Mosquito squadron had a particularly hard time towards the end of the war when often the same planes were used for two operational sorties in a day. As soon as possible each plane was partly refuelled. This meant filling just the main tanks for, as the destination of the next operation was not yet known, the amount of petrol required could not be determined at this early stage. The smaller tanks were filled up, as necessary, just before an 'op'.

Frequently planes came back peppered with holes from anti-aircraft flak or from fighter cannon. Stirling H-Harry (EE884) was one such case. It was coned by searchlights on its way to bomb Mulheim in June 1943. The bomber was still some distance short of its target when an engine packed up after being hit by flak. The pilot decided to dump his bomb-load and get away from the glare of the searchlights and return to England. He managed to do this and made an emergency landing at East Wretham, near Thetford. When the crew inspected the aircraft later they found that it had no fewer than eighty-eight flak holes in it.

Sometimes a fault or mechanical defect prevented the bombs being dropped and then the plane had to be brought back and landed with its highly explosive load still hung up. A Stirling could carry up to six 500 lb bombs inside its wings, but if one got stuck it was very difficult to extricate because of its awkward position and the distance between the wing and the ground.

***LAC Bill J.A. Overton, 218 Squadron***: On a couple of occasions our Stirling came back with 250 lb bombs hung-up inside its wings. In order to get them safely down, we inflated air-bags under the wing. The armourer then crawled into the wing bomb-bay and did whatever was

*Air and groundcrew, with a proud 'Chiefie' in the middle, sit on the wing of 218 Squadron's Stirling EF133 A-Able early in 1944.* Len Taylor, via John Reid

necessary to release the bomb. At the same time we had to carefully open the bomb-door manually and thus the bomb was wangled out onto the soft, pneumatic air-bag. The aircraft was then towed away, the air-bag deflated and everybody beat a hasty retreat while the armourers were left to their own devices to make the bomb safe.

Severe weather conditions during the flight could also cause bombs to hang up without the crew even realizing what had happened until they got back to base. One such occasion has been recorded by Flight Lieutenant Murray Peden, DFC, a Canadian pilot of a Stirling in 214 Squadron.

On the way in, we flew through some extremely heavy icing; but we struggled clear after a short time and thought no more about it. We flew A-Able back to Downham Market . . . where we got a bit of a surprise in our own dispersal. One of the groundcrew went through the normal drill with me after I had positioned the aircraft, calling up to me to ask if we had any hang-ups. I double checked with J.B., who assured me that every green light had come on, indicating proper circuits and clear drops for every bomb. I shouted down to the chappie standing beyond the nose, confirming that we had no hang-ups. 'Righto,' he said 'open the bomb doors.' I flicked the bomb door switch, and a moment later he walked in underneath to give the bomb-bay the usual perfunctory visual check. Hardly had he disappeared than I saw him come pelting out in front again hollering for help in excited tones. I pricked up my ears and learned that we still had a 500-pounder aboard, adhering to the bomb-bay only by virtue of a thin film of ice . . . without benefit of debate or discussion we all made a hasty and undignified exit.[31]

Occasionally planes returned with bombs on board for other reasons, such as inability to locate the target accurately.

**F/Sgt Johnny P.G. Baines, 635 Squadron**: We had one or two problems when we returned to Downham Market after a daylight operation to Wessel. This was for the army, but on arriving over the target there was low cloud and the Master Bomber cancelled the attack and we had to bring our bombs back. On landing we were well down the runway and, with the extra weight, the brakes wouldn't stop the aircraft. So the pilot swung the plane onto the grass at the side of the runway and the wing-tip touched the ground. I thought it would turn over, so I opened the turret doors to jump out, but it righted again.

But it was not only bombs which posed problems for returning crews. Even if the aircraft had come back unscathed a landing could still be made difficult by the conditions encountered at the airfield. On the night of 15 December 1944, for instance, two 635 Squadron Lancasters turned wide at the end of the runway and got bogged down in the soft grass because the flarepath lights were not working and the edge of the runway could not be seen in the dark.

A change in the weather could also, of course, create difficulties. Fog was always to be feared, enveloping everything, as it does, in disorientating invisibility. Even when FIDO was brought into use to clear away the pervasive fog, landing a heavy aircraft was still a chancy thing to bring off successfully.

**P/O Reg Davey**: We only used it once but it was a most hairy experience. Our Stirling lurched all over the place as we hit the glare and it was a nightmare at the end of the runway in the fog waiting for a lighted truck to guide us and expecting another aircraft in our back at any moment.

During the winter of 1944/45 bad weather persisted for weeks on end, but because of the dangerous situation created by the German offensive in the Ardennes it became imperative to continue the air support for allied troops in Belgium. As a result FIDO had to be used many

*A Lancaster takes off with the aid of FIDO. Mostly FIDO was used for aircraft returning from raids in thick fog and more than 160 planes landed at Downham Market with its help.* Imperial War Museum CH15272

times at Downham during that difficult period. One memorable occasion was on the afternoon of Christmas Eve when the pipelines were set alight to assist the take-off for an attack on Düsseldorf airfield. By the time of the squadron's return the fog was, if anything, worse. But by the aid of FIDO – which had been kept burning for many hours – the squadron and fifteen 'cuckoos', including a Flying Fortress, were enabled to land without mishap.

The turbulence caused by the heat from the tunnel of flames, together with the fear of what might happen should the flames manage to ignite any petrol leaking from a plane, made landing with FIDO a somewhat unnerving business.

*W/Cdr Peter McDermott, DFC, DFM, 608 Squadron*: I well remember my first landing with it. There was low cloud and fog and we were warned as we crossed the coast that FIDO was in use. It soon became obvious – a glow through the cloud, a heat-induced miniature cumulus cloud above the airfield lit up like a giant Chinese lantern, and other aircraft clearly visible as they circled at their allocated heights awaiting their turn to land. Landing was rather slower than normal, so we had time to ponder on what was in store and try to remember what we had been told about variation from the usual (landing) technique. Then we were called in, preliminary flap down-wind, turn in towards the glow and then in the cloud and fog. A burst of light as we came over the bar, and then there was this tunnel of less misty area ahead with intense flames on each side from the petroleum burners. It was quite a sight as we ran along to the end of the runway before turning off into relative gloom and then mist again.

Added to the difficulties of returning crews was the danger from enemy intruders. Although no aircraft from Downham's own squadrons were ever directly attacked by intruders while landing the fear was always present that it could happen, particularly as crews received warnings from time to time of intruders in the vicinity. In fact, the airfield itself was attacked a number of

*A Mosquito takes off with the aid of FIDO.* Imperial War Museum CH15273

times by German aircraft but only twice was any damage inflicted. On one occasion, in the early hours of the morning of 24 August 1943, the airfield was attacked as part of a German diversionary tactic to a planned raid on Hull. Three high explosive bombs were dropped during the attack making a crater in one of the runways. Over a hundred little butterfly bombs – each equipped with tiny wings which caused the weapon to explode when touched – were also dropped over the airfield and on the Bexwell Road part of Downham Market. Most of 218 and 623 Squadrons' returning aircraft were diverted to other airfields, but one plane with two wounded men on board managed to land at Downham soon after the attack.

**LAC Len Warner, 623 Squadron**: Then we saw an aircraft fly down the runway about 250 feet up. Ah well, he'll go round again we thought. Down came the next 623 kite and bang – the tail wheel burst! As the tail wheel was solid rubber on some Stirlings – strange we thought! Word came that there was an enemy aircraft about. When the bods went to guide the kite with the damaged tail-wheel to dispersal they saw anti-personnel bombs about. We spent the rest of the night driving an old David Brown tractor up and down the runway – looking, with torches, for the bombs. We lashed pipes to the tractor, put up sheet metal in front of the driver complete with a slit for him to see where he was going and in this way we destroyed quite a number of these bombs. The next day they cleared away those that had gone on the grass.

Those anti-personnel bombs which had fallen in the grass were cleared away by dragging a heavy chain between two lorries and those which had fallen in the woods were shot with Sten-guns to explode them.

A further enemy attack on the airfield took place the following month. It was late in the evening, on 6 September, and the runway lights were on when, at about ten o'clock, the Control Tower was advised of an intruder. It was bright moonlight and apparently a visiting aircraft was in the circuit, waiting to land, when a twin-engined Messerschmitt Me 410 flew in fast at 400 feet and dropped a 250 kg high explosive bomb on the runway. Two airmen were slightly injured.

And then, of course, there were all the landings made doubly difficult due to crew injuries or damage sustained while on operations. Too often these perilous landings ended up as crash-landings, sometimes with fatal results. In one instance I-Item, a Stirling of 218 Squadron, had been caught by flak over Bochum on 14 May 1943 and only managed to get back to Downham Market the following morning with great difficulty.

**Sgt Len W.J. Durrant, 218 Squadron**: We made an almost normal approach despite the vibration which threatened to disintegrate the aircraft. On landing, however, the brakes failed and the aircraft swung off the runway, heading for the Operations Building. A few yards short of the building was an air-raid shelter and the Stirling seemed to run up the curved side of the shelter and then took off again before crashing into the side of the Operations Building. One engine caught fire but that was quickly extinguished. Apart from the expected cuts and bruises none of the crew suffered any injury. We were all examined by the Medical Officer and given a sedative which must have been rather strong as I have no recollection of the remainder of the 14th May and very little of the 15th!

Unfortunately, two aircrew from another plane, who had just landed and were entering the building for interrogation, were killed in the accident.

On the same raid G-George was attacked by an enemy fighter shortly after crossing the

*Stirling I-Item of 218 Squadron crashed near the station's Operations Block on 14 May 1943.* L.W.J. Durrant

Belgian border. The rear-gunner was killed and the aircraft severely damaged, but the pilot, Sergeant T.J. Nichols, managed to get the plane back to England and then, running short of fuel, made for Chedburgh for an emergency landing. As they came in to land it was found that the flaps and undercarriage were inoperative and just before the pilot could execute a wheels-up landing all the engines cut out and the aircraft crashed near the airfield killing four more of the crew and badly injuring Nichols.[32]

Many crashes took place near, but beyond the confines of the airfield. They included different types of aircraft from airfields all over East Anglia. The airfield's fire officer was required to keep a record of all crashes dealt with by Downham Market. According to the fire officer, Flying Officer W.F. Provis, during one six-month period they dealt with twenty-one crashes.

The men of the local depot of the National Fire Service, as it was then called, were also kept very busy. A graphic description of an emergency call and a typical dash to a crashed bomber was given to the local newspaper just before the end of the war by Mr Twyman, a former Company Officer of the Downham depot.

> Then men of Downham moved without wasting a second. Up Priory Road, or down Railway Road, out of town, men dressing inside the tender and preparing the equipment, with the speedometer registering 60 or more on the straight. Then open fen at night, only a white ribbon of road in the headlights that seemed to race under the wheels like a bumpy tape; all around the black void, and, ahead, the blaze. The sudden extra impulse of the jump of the tender as the driver gives the gas for the run up to the scene; the brilliant white flashes of exploding ammunition interspersed the mass of red, and the swirls and flurries of heavy, oily black smoke, left no time to ask questions. The men knew their job: first the crew, second the fire.[33]

During the autumn of 1944 there was a spate of accidents to returning Mosquitos of 608 Squadron. Quite a few of the squadron's planes were obliged to make forced landings at the

Woodbridge and Manston emergency landing grounds between August and November. An attempted landing at Downham itself on 9 October ended in disaster when a Mosquito hit the tower of Stow Bardolph Hall and crashed at Wimbotsham. On 6 November another Mosquito became iced up and crashed at Boardswell. In both cases the crews were killed.

Fortunately, some of the crews managed to survive even the calamitous return flights when everything that could go wrong did go wrong.

*F/Lt Peter S. Hobbs, DFC, 608 Squadron*: On another occasion we were returning from northern Germany [Karlsruhe] when our Mosquito lost an engine. We were below cloud, which meant we could not see the stars, so to make certain we were not heading towards Russia, I asked Jake to call 'Manston Emergency' as a check that we were flying westwards. Our radar boxes and distant reading compass were u/s, they normally being driven by our now dead engine. Manston took no chances and called us every quarter of an hour or so, eventually saying: 'Fly 215, and proceed to Bradwell Bay.' At Bradwell they gave us landing instructions and said, 'If you swing on landing, swing to starboard.' It was our starboard engine that was dead. We landed; we swung to starboard! We broke the FIDO pipeline, careered through an air-raid shelter, a hedge, a herd of cows and ended up fifty yards from what to me looked like the beach. It was, in fact, the outline of the FIDO installation fuel tank containing thousands of gallons of petrol. We climbed out; the ambulance-men eventually

*F/Lt P.S. Hobbs, DFC, and F/Lt C. R. Jacobs, DFC, of 608 Squadron, pictured with their Mosquito on the morning after completing the last (50th) sortie of their second tour in April 1945. Notice the bundle of 'Window' near the aircraft's starboard wheel ready for the next night's operation. C.R. Jacobs*

arrived, saying they didn't know where we had disappeared to, and so had been unable to find us. So unhurt, we left the cows to their placid grazing.

Downham served as an emergency landing ground on more than one occasion. In one notable incident, during December 1943, a Lancaster of 97 Squadron landed on two engines at the airfield after it had been hit while flying over Berlin by incendiary bombs from another aircraft flying above it.

Perhaps the most memorable return, however, was that of Lancaster D-Dog of 635 Squadron on 6 October 1944. The squadron had dispatched six of its aircraft from RAF Downham Market to bomb the Scholven Buer oil-plant at Gelsenkirchen and all of the planes had been hit by flak. D-Dog had been hit over Holland on its way to the target and trouble developed in the port inner engine so that the plane could not gain any height. Over the target, and just after releasing its bombs, the plane was hit again and the port inner engine caught fire. The fire was extinguished and the pilot, Flight Lieutenant Alex Thorne, DSO, DFC, set course for home with only three engines working. Over the Dutch coast the Lancaster was hit yet again by flak. This time part of the starboard rudder was shot away and the port outer engine failed. The aircraft rapidly lost height and an S.O.S. was sent out to warn the coastal patrol that they intended ditching the plane in the North Sea. When the English coast was eventually sighted the S.O.S. was cancelled and Thorne headed for the emergency airfield at Woodbridge. As they approached the airfield at about 500 feet the starboard inner engine packed up, leaving only one engine working. D-Dog swerved to port but the pilot managed to put the plane into a glide and made a successful landing in a field near the airfield. As the crew climbed out the ammunition started exploding and soon the aircraft was burning furiously. All managed to escape from the blazing inferno except the wireless operator Sergeant Jim Crabtree, whose body was later found amongst the charred remains of the plane. Thorne lost consciousness immediately after staggering onto the ground. The next thing he remembered was 'waking up in a wood to which the crew had taken him on the boundary of the field. With them was a lady who had hurried over from her nearby farmhouse, undeterred by the explosions still erupting from the burning D-Dog. She asked them if they would like some tea. She hurried back to her home and soon returned with what must have been her best tea-set on a silver tray with a white lace cover.'[34]

# CHAPTER 8

# Missing

An aircrew which managed to finish its tour of thirty or so sorties was likely to be feeling a bit isolated at the end of the tour. Very few of the other aircrews who were on the airfield at the start of the tour six months earlier would still be there. Some would have already finished their tours and gone elsewhere. Most, however, never finished their tours. Indeed, for the greater part of the war the chances of an aircrew completing their first tour, let alone a second tour, were very slim.

> ***Sgt Maxie Booth, 218 Squadron***: We lived two crews per Nissen hut. On the day that we arrived the other crew was just leaving the Nissen hut to go out on ops as we moved in. Early next morning the Military Police came to collect that crew's gear – 'Missing on Ops!' This was our initiation. But a new crew was installed with us within the next twenty-four hours. That was just the way of life in those days.

Only in the last few months of the war was there much hope of survival for aircrews.

Aircrews who went out on an op and failed to return were posted as Missing. The very word 'missing', whilst being strictly accurate, carried ominous overtones. On the one hand, it gave a degree of hope – hope that the plane was simply overdue and might still return later; hope that the plane had, unknown to anyone, landed at another airfield; or hope that the crew had, in some miraculous way, been able to escape from their doomed plane and would, eventually, turn up. But, at the same time, there was an instinctive feeling that if the plane had not returned by a certain time then it would, almost certainly, never return. A knowledge that the plane was lost forever and that all its crew had been killed; killed, moreover, in horrible ways – killed, perhaps, as the plane crashed into the ground, or as it was shot to pieces in the sky, or killed when parachutes failed to open.

Most of the Missing were, in fact, killed in action. In all, some 144 Stirlings and Lancasters, each carrying crews of seven airmen, failed to return and fourteen Mosquitos, with crews of two each, suffered similar fates. Probably 850 airmen, or more, were killed in action whilst flying out of Downham.[35] Most of the remainder – perhaps another 150 airmen – became prisoners-of-war. Only a few of the airmen who had been shot down were able to escape from enemy hands. Many of those who ended up in prison camps had also been badly wounded. In addition, of course, there were the many airmen who were wounded in action when their planes were hit but still, somehow, managed to return to Britain in their stricken aircraft.

During the first two months of operations losses from Downham Market had been appallingly high; in this period fourteen aircraft failed to return from only twenty-two raids. On one raid to Hamburg in July three aircraft had been lost and on another night in August four aircraft went missing while laying mines in Kiel Harbour. The loss-rate for this period in 1942 worked out as one aircraft for every twelve sorties and, as the aircrew were expected to complete thirty sorties on their first tour and another twenty on their second tour, the chance of any surviving at this rate of attrition was absolutely minimal. Fortunately things began to improve during the latter part of 1942 and the loss-rate was reduced to one aircraft for every twenty sorties. This still meant, in practice, that only a

*'Missing on Ops'. The Operations Board for 24 August 1942 shows aircraft from 115 Squadron and 218 Squadron detailed for the raid on Frankfurt. R-Roger, one of the nine Stirlings from 218 Squadron at Downham Market, failed to return from the raid and has been posted as* MISSING *on the Board. L.E Skan, via John Reid*

third of all aircrews could expect to survive a first tour and less than 10 per cent could expect to survive both tours. It remained far too high a loss-rate, but at least it was an improvement in the right direction.

A year later conditions had deteriorated once again and during this period, in June 1943, seven Stirlings of 218 Squadron were lost within the space of five nights. It was into this situation that Eleanor Bignall, a teleprinter operator, was thrown in 1943 when she transferred from 3 Group Headquarters at Exning to the Signals Section at Downham.

**Eleanor Zaleski (nee Cpl Bignall), WAAF**: Immediately I set foot in the Signals Section I was given the awful job of sending fourteen telegrams to next-of-kin: 'We deeply regret to inform you, etc.' But later on that evening, I had the happy duty of sending seven telegrams saying that the aircraft (i.e. one of the two missing aircraft) had been diverted to Scotland and all [had] safely landed.

The majority of aircraft that failed to return just went missing. How or where they met their end was rarely known at the time as it was impossible to identify which aircraft had been hit at any particular location during a night raid. The place where the bomber crashed was, of course, recorded by the enemy when they went to collect the wreckage. Sometimes the story of the last minutes of a bomber's flight can be pieced together from these and other records. In this way the fate of Stirling D-Dog (BK712) has been painstakingly reconstructed by Alfred Price.

D-Dog, piloted by Pilot Officer W.G. Shillinglaw, took off from Downham just after midnight on 21/22 June 1943, on its way to bomb Krefeld.

The assembly point was Aldeburgh, on the Suffolk coast. From there the bombers were to fly south-east, on a heading of one-zero-five degrees, straight to Krefeld. As Shillinglaw's Stirling left the coast of East Anglia behind it, the gunners each fired a short burst to test their guns. Now both pilot and gunners settled down to the deadly serious business of each scanning his allotted piece of the sky for lurking night-fighters. The three-quarters full moon gave the crewmen a distinct feeling of nakedness. Then the crew of Tomtit's long-range Freya radar (situated 15 miles north-east of Brussels) observed a lone aircraft which, if it held its present course, would run right into the range of their precision radars. All this was unknown to the men on board D-Dog. For some reason Shillinglaw and his crew strayed over Belgium and now, at 0115 hours, they were moving east-wards on Krefeld. But between them and their target was radar station Tomtit. Orbiting over Tomtit in a Messerschmitt Bf 110 was Leutnant Heinz-Wolfgang Schnaufer. A half minute before the two aircraft, flying on almost opposite headings, crossed, Kuhnel (in the radar station Tomtit) directed Schnaufer to turn to starboard through almost half a circle. The Messerschmitt pilot followed these instructions precisely, and slid in neatly behind the Stirling and its unsuspecting crew. As Schnaufer closed in underneath the bomber he was seen by one of the Stirling's gunners, and Shillinglaw hurled his aircraft into a violent corkscrew in an effort to shake off his pursuer. But in vain, the German pilot closed in to 50 yards, firing his powerful battery of cannon and machine-guns whenever he managed to get the twisting bomber within his sights. The Stirling crumpled under the impact of exploding shells, then the fuselage and wings burst into flames. Mortally wounded, the bomber flew on for a short time, then plunged earthwards.[36]

None of the seven-man crew survived the crash and the subsequent fire. Schnaufer later became the Luftwaffe's top-scoring nightfighter pilot with 121 'kills' to his credit.

Occasionally, of course, some of the crew escaped from a stricken plane and it was possible to find out later what exactly had happened when the aircraft had gone missing. The truth, when discovered, was rarely very palatable, especially when tragedy was the result of an accident that might have been avoided. Stirling H-Harry (EE909) had flown eight sorties for 218 Squadron when both it and its crew were transferred to Downham's fledgling 623 Squadron. On 28 August 1943 H-Harry was shot down while returning from a raid on Nuremberg. The aircraft had been attacked by an enemy fighter just after bombing the target, but, not being seriously damaged, the pilot, Pilot Officer G.L. Jenkins, DFC, started taking evasive action and began corkscrewing the plane. Unfortunately, this must have appeared aggressive for a Halifax taking part in the same raid fired on the Stirling and the port wing caught fire. Six members of the crew managed to bale out and were taken prisoner, but the pilot was trapped in his seat and died when the plane crashed at Birkenfeld.

All losses were shocks but morale, nevertheless, remained high. Sometimes, however, the loss of an aircrew was felt even more heavily than usual due to special circumstances. One such occasion was on 24 July 1943 when Hamburg was raided and 'Window' was used for the first time to cause havoc among the defenders. Because of the importance of this raid a maximum effort was called for. Altogether 218 Squadron managed to send twenty aircraft led by its Australian commanding officer Wing Commander D.T. Saville, DFC. At thirty-nine years of age Saville was probably the oldest RAF pilot still flying on operations; he was certainly one of the most experienced with thousands of hours' commercial flying behind him and a veteran of fifty-four operational sorties. Don Saville's method of commanding was to lead by example and to take part in the most difficult raids.

On the night in question Saville asked for volunteers to join his crew as most of his regulars had moved on after the expiry of their own tours. The scratch crew that he got together were mostly on their second tour and included the Squadron Signals Officer, Flight Lieutenant Stanley as wireless operator, and the Station Gunnery Officer, Flight Lieutenant Birbeck as mid-upper gunner. In addition, there was an eighth crewman, Flight Sergeant Bevis, as second pilot – presumably getting experience at the start of his tour of operations. Saville's Stirling was shot down by a fighter over the outskirts of Hamburg just as he was beginning his bombing run. Of the eight-man crew only one – Flying Officer Eyre, the bomb-aimer – managed to escape alive. Thus three of the 218 Squadron's leaders were lost at a single blow. Apparently three more airmen managed to parachute from the aircraft but they were lynched as they landed and then hanged from lamp-posts by a civilian mob incensed by the mass destruction of their city. Eyre escaped the fury of the mob because he had landed on an airfield building and fortuitously fell directly into the hands of the Luftwaffe. Saville was posthumously awarded the Distinguished Service Order for his services to the squadron.

In April 1944 a similar fate befell 635 Squadron when it lost its commanding officer Wing Commander A. G. S. Cousens, DSO, DFC. Cousens had taken charge of the new squadron when it was formed a month earlier and, according to an anonymous author writing soon after the war, 'much of the Squadron's later success may be attributed to the fine spirit inculcated by this navigator/Squadron Commander.'[37] On 18 April, less than a month after its formation, 635 Squadron was asked to provide a Master Bomber for a raid on the railway marshalling yards at Rouen in northern France. This job fell to Cousens flying with his pilot Flight Lieutenant Courtenay. No aircraft were lost on this raid but extensive damage was done to the railway yards. Then on 22 April Cousens took on the role of Master Bomber for the third successive raid, this time to control the northern wave of an attack on Laon's marshalling yards. 'Although his aiming instructions were clearly heard throughout the attack, his aircraft failed to return to base. Six months later the pilot reached England after having been liberated by the Americans. From Courtenay it was learned that the aircraft had been attacked by an unseen fighter fifteen minutes after leaving the target. The aircraft immediately exploded.'[38] Cousens and all the rest of the crew, apart from Courtenay, who had been thrown from the plane, were immediately killed. (For details of Courtenay's escape see page 98.)

Tremendous bravery was often shown by the airmen even when severely wounded. Most of these tales of courage and devotion will never be known, their unheard-of acts of valour being lost with the deaths of their unsung heroes. Occasionally epics of bravery have been reported by those who survived and have become well known. On such is the story of Flight Sergeant Arthur Aaron's last flight which is worth re-telling here as a symbol for all.

Arthur Aaron took off from Downham, along with twelve other aircraft, on 12 August 1943 to bomb Turin in northern Italy. Just as he was approaching the target at 9,000 feet his Stirling was sprayed with machine-gun fire. The navigator had been killed instantly and several of the crew were wounded including the twenty-one year old pilot who, bleeding profusely, slumped across his seat onto the joy-stick. The flight engineer was later to recall the situation.

*Sgt Malcolm Mitchem, 218 Squadron*: The whole cockpit was hidden in deep shadow. Then I realized we were getting into a steep dive. Our speed was increasing rapidly. I wondered why he (Aaron) was doing nothing to stop it. But then, as we turned away from the moon, the light streamed in and I could see his face. It was a dreadful sight. He had been hit in the side of the face. His oxygen mask had gone and I thought that the whole of his jaw had been shot off. His right arm was almost severed at the elbow and he had been wounded in the chest. Yet somehow, despite his terrible injuries, he had the forethought to signal to me to take over.[39]

*F/Sgt Arthur Aaron, VC, of 218 Squadron, photographed when he was an aircrew cadet. He was posthumously awarded the Victoria Cross for conspicuous bravery on the night of 12/13 August 1943, after a raid on Turin, Italy.* Imperial War Museum CH11680

Mitchem took over the controls and, although wounded in the leg himself, succeeded in righting the bomber before it began to spin out of control and levelled it at about 3,000 feet. Then Mitchem handed over the controls to the bomb-aimer Allan Larden, while he went to inspect the damage. The windscreen was shattered, one engine was useless, both the front and rear gun-turrets had been put out of action and the wing controls damaged. In addition, and unknown to the crew, they still carried on board a 4,000 lb bomb and the undercarriage was damaged. It was not possible to climb back over the Alps and return home so they headed south towards the Mediterranean instead. Meanwhile Aaron had been moved from the pilot's seat to the rear of the plane where he was laid on the floor and treated with morphine. Drifting between a semi-conscious dream-world and reality Aaron managed to give some instructions to his crew by writing on a small pad with his left hand. Five hours after leaving the target they reached the North African coast and made contact with the airfield at Bone, in Tunisia. Aaron, though at the limit of exhaustion and in great pain, insisted on being taken back to his seat where he tried to land the damaged bomber in the dark. Three times, flying with one hand and in the full force of the slipstream coming in through the broken windscreen, Aaron attempted to land the plane. Then, as Aaron's remaining strength ebbed away and fuel was fast running out, the controls were taken again by Larden who landed the Stirling safely with its wheels up and with its bomb still on board.

It is possible that Aaron might have recovered if he had been content to lie still and conserve his strength. In fact, he died nine hours after the hazardous landing. He was posthumously awarded the Victoria Cross, the citation of which stated that 'in appalling conditions he showed the greatest qualities of courage, determination and leadership, and, though wounded and dying, he set an example of devotion to duty which has seldom been equalled and never surpassed.'[40] The bomb-aimer Allan Larden was awarded the Conspicuous Gallantry Medal, and the wireless operator Jimmy Guy and the flight engineer Malcolm Mitchem were each awarded the Distinguished Flying Medal for their part in helping to bring back the aircraft safely. Unfortunately, the two gunners received nothing, as the squadron gunnery leader who would have recommended them was killed in action. Ironically, it was later established that the gunfire which had caused so much damage had accidentally come from another Stirling (but not from 218 Squadron) taking part in the raid.

A year later a second Victoria Cross was won by a pilot stationed at Downham. On 4 August 1944 fourteen Lancasters of 635 Squadron took part in a raid on a V1 depot at Trossy-St-Maxim in northern France. The target had been bombed on both of the previous days so the enemy were ready and the attacking force consequently came under heavy anti-aircraft fire. Two of 635 Squadron's planes were shot down and a further eight of the squadron's aircraft were damaged by flak. As Squadron Leader Ian W. Bazalgette's Lancaster approached the target it was caught in the barrage of fire. The bomb-aimer, Flight Lieutenant I.A. Hibbert, was seriously injured, two engines were put out of action and the starboard wing and the fuselage were set on fire. As the Deputy Master Bomber, Flight Lieutenant R.W. Beveridge, had already been shot down even before he could mark the target Bazalgette realized that it was essential for him, as the Primary Visual Marker in the attack, to mark the target if the raid was to achieve its purpose. So he pressed on to the aiming point while the rest of his crew tried to put out the fires. He successfully marked the target, but after releasing the target indicators and bombs the plane became almost unmanageable and it went into a spin.

*S/Ldr Ian Willoughby Bazalgette, VC, DFC, of 635 Squadron. His Victoria Cross was awarded posthumously for conspicuous bravery on 4 August 1944, during a raid on Trossy St Maxim, France.* Imperial War Museum CH15911

Somehow, by superhuman effort and expert airmanship, Bazalgette was able to regain control of the aircraft. Then, thirty miles after leaving the target, a third engine failed and the mid-upper gunner, Flight Sergeant V.V.R. Leeder, was overcome by smoke fumes. After confirming that he would try to crash-land the plane and thus save the wounded men, Bazalgette ordered the rest of his crew to bale out, which they successfully did from only 1,000 feet up. By then the blazing Lancaster was approaching the village of Senantes. With great skill Bazalgette attempted the almost hopeless task of landing the crippled plane. He managed to veer away from the village and safely crash-landed in a nearby field. But it was all to no avail for before any assistance could be given the aircraft exploded and its three remaining occupants were instantly killed.

The people of Senantes, who had witnessed Bazalgette's outstanding act of bravery, were full of praise for him and the way in which he had avoided their village. They turned out in his honour and the Mayor wrote a letter of sympathy to the pilot's mother. When the remaining crew eventually got back to England the full story was unravelled and Squadron Leader Bazalgette was posthumously awarded the Victoria Cross. 'His heroic sacrifice marked', according to the official citation, 'the climax of a long career of operations against the enemy. He always chose the more dangerous and exacting roles. His courage and devotion to duty were beyond praise.'[41]

For those who survived it was impossible to ignore the risks attached to each and every operation and impossible also to forget the fate of colleagues who had succumbed to those risks.

*P/O Reg Davey, 218 Squadron*: One of the worst things after a raid was getting into bed – probably at around 4 am, still strung up with a stomach in turmoil – and you were just dozing

*Telegram sent to Sgt L. Ashplant's mother informing her that her son, of 623 Squadron, had gone 'missing' on an operation the previous night, 18 November 1943. L. Ashplant, via Steve C. Smith*

off when the Military Police burst in to the hut to ask where so and so's bed was as he had not come back and they had to take away his possessions for security reasons. It was most upsetting if you had struck up a friendship with the lad; but we kidded ourselves that he was safe and would see the end of the war in a German prisoner-of-war camp.

When any aircrew went missing there was then the unpleasant duties to be done of sorting out their kit.

**Mrs J. Pointer (nee Smith), WAAF**: Another difficult task we had was notifying relatives when aircrew didn't return. Sometimes the telegrams would come up in batches, there were so many. I remember after Nuremberg it was particularly unpleasant.[42]

The job of letting relatives know fell mainly to the Padre and his staff. They needed to be extremely careful because often a WAAF on the camp had become friendly with an airman who had gone missing. There was no point in causing unnecessary suffering by informing the WAAF before the facts were known, but sometimes it was difficult to avoid rumours being spread around. Serious relationships between opposite sexes were, in any case, discouraged; for relationships led to marriages and today's wife could so easily become tomorrow's widow.

For the survivors of an operation there was often the duty to visit the next-of-kin of missing aircrew.

**Sgt Pat Nolan, 635 Squadron**: I had the unenviable task of visiting the next-of-kin of some of the crew. What I found most embarrassing was the fact that in all cases they seemed to be afraid or reluctant to talk about the circumstances of their son's death. I think it was in deference to my feelings; whereas I would have preferred to have given them a detailed account of the event.

## CHAPTER 9
# Capture and Evasion

Amongst the Missing were those that somehow managed to escape from their burning and exploding planes by parachuting down to safety. What happened afterwards – whether they landed softly or broke some bones, or whether they fell into the hands of riotous mobs, the dreaded Gestapo or the more understanding military – was often simply a matter of luck. There was, in any case, very little that a parachuting airman could do to alter the course of subsequent events: he was a victim of circumstances beyond his control.

Navigator Ian Robb, for instance, was in luck at first when he baled out of his stricken plane on the night of 30 August 1943. He had been on his eighth 'op' when his Stirling was shot down by a nightfighter over Mönchengladbach. Three of the crew, including Robb, managed to escape from the plane before it crashed near Dorplein, Holland; the remaining four were all killed. Robb immediately fell into the friendly hands of the Resistance and was passed by them across Belgium, via Liege and Brussels, and into France as far as Paris.

*Sgt Ian A. Robb, 218 Squadron*: At the time the Germans had wiped out the escape route south to the Pyrenees, so I was sent east again to a small town called Fismes, near Reims, with the idea of being air-lifted out. Unfortunately, the group was betrayed and we were all arrested by the Gestapo on 31 December. I was held in Reims prison until the end of May 1944 when the Americans bombed the railway yards behind the gaol and also hit one end of the gaol enabling five prisoners to escape. I was then moved to Chalons-sur-Marne and later moved up to Fresnes prison, near Paris. This final move was the normal practice for airmen caught in 'civvies' in France. Early in August, as the Americans were advancing on Paris, we were all put aboard a cattle-truck and finished up in Buchenwald concentration camp. We remained there until October when I was sent to Stalag Luft III.

Many other airmen fell almost immediately into the hands of the enemy. Such was the fate of the crew of E-Easy, one of three Stirlings that failed to return to Downham on the night of 18 November 1943 from a raid on Mannheim. E-Easy had been coned by searchlights and hit by heavy flak before arriving at the target, and rear-gunner Frank Matthews was soaked in oil as the pipe leads to his turret were fractured. With two engines on fire and losing height the bombs were quickly dropped in an attempt to keep flying, but to no avail. The pilot then gave the order to abandon the plane over Mönchengladbach.

*Sgt Frank Matthews, 623 Squadron*: I fixed my parachute and jettisoned the turret doors, pressed both feet on the back plates of the guns and bailed out. The aircraft seemed to be well on fire as flames were burning in the slipstream from the fractured fuel tanks and caused a sort of vacuum which hindered the downward drift of the 'chute. I landed in a ploughed field. There were a couple of inches of snow and [it was] very cold. I eventually came to a small road and was able to hide the 'chute in a ditch. After this I met up with my wireless op. Sgt Milnthorpe [and] we managed to find a small coppice or wood and waited for daylight. When at last dawn approached we looked over the surrounding fields; there were dozens of

Volksturm, some with dogs, who, within a very short time, had found us. We were handed over to the Luftwaffe officer. He escorted us to Stalag Luft 3.

E-Easy continued flying for another 3 miles before crashing and bursting into flames again. The fire was eventually put out and the Stirling was put under guard. Apparently, it was the first four-engined bomber to crash in the area and during the next few days many officials visited the site to photograph the Stirling and strip its fittings for further examination.

It was not just fear of imprisonment which drove allied airmen to evade the enemy. Not long after the Hamburg raids of July 1943 Goering had declared that any British aircrew captured would be treated without mercy and shot as murderers.

*P/O Reg Davey, 218 Squadron*: You can imagine that had an effect on morale and, as a sweetener, we were all issued with a revolver and six bullets. I got a Smith-Wesson 45, which terrified me and I hid it in the bottom of my chest-of-drawers and carried on with packing extra food down my battle-dress, as I figured that that would be of more use to me if shot down. Some men did fly with their revolvers and I remember that we had some Canadians carrying guns, daggers and ropes around their waists. It was frightening to realize that, on returning from a booze-up in the town, men would sometimes let off steam by shooting holes in the corrugated iron roof of a Nissen hut; the damage was usually not noticed until the next time it rained!

On a rare occasion an airman might survive even without his parachute. One such fortunate airman was Bill Jackson, the rear-gunner and only survivor of a Stirling. The aircraft had left

*Remains of Stirling E-Easy of 218 Squadron after crashing near Mönchengladbach, 18 November 1943.*
Steve C. Smith.

Downham in the early evening of 27 January 1943 and had flown across Denmark to lay mines in the Baltic Sea. After dropping three mines successfully the fourth mine refused to budge. Weather conditions continued to deteriorate and it was decided to return home by flying low over northern Germany and then attempt to release the mine 'safe' over the North Sea. Somewhere north of Hannover the giant aircraft suddenly ran into the side of a hill and immediately exploded.

*W/O Bill Jackson, 218 Squadron*: I do not remember when I finally shot out of the turret, but I know I passed through a terrific explosion as the 'hung up' mine exploded. I didn't hear it, but the flash was to remain with me forever. Round and round I went, head over heels, seemingly dropping slowly from a great altitude. Then I was crashing through the tree tops and seemed to bounce from branch to branch until I was deposited in a heap of snow between two large tree trunks. When I awoke, only small pieces of the [Stirling's] fuselage remained. Huge pine trees were now blazing like gigantic torches, some splitting from top to bottom with ear-shattering cracks and shedding millions of burning splinters in every direction. My rear turret was nowhere to be seen, but a small portion of the fuselage was still stubbornly resisting the flames. I circled the wreckage time and time again, ploughing my way painfully through the thick snow, falling down and picking myself up, getting so near to the burning debris that I could smell the scorching of my own hair. I called for the boys again and again. But no answer came to my ears.[43]

After a rest Jackson eventually set off through the forest in the direction of the Dutch border. It was only after walking a mile in the snow that he realized that his feet were going numb and, looking down, saw that he wasn't wearing anything on his feet. Painfully Jackson made his way back through the forest to the scene of the crash, hoping to find his boots. Instead, he found a German policeman waiting for him.

Bomber Command lost ninety-five of its aircraft in a single night during the disastrous raid on Nuremberg on 30 March 1944. Three of the Lancasters shot down were from 635 Squadron; in two of the planes all the aircrew were killed. The third aircraft, T-Tommy, was hit by flak near Koblenz and fared somewhat better, five of its seven-man crew managing to escape and later become prisoners. One of these was wireless operator William Ogilvie who was captured and imprisoned in a number of different camps, and survived the long forced-march across eastern Germany during the exceptionally bitter winter at the beginning of 1945.

*F/Sgt William D. Ogilvie, 635 Squadron*: For this raid we were in the Primary Blind Markers again. A new tactic was being tried out – a variable zero hour. A number of aircraft were to radio their exact positions and wind directions back to base in code, but it meant breaking radio silence during the flight. The raid was like any other as far as the coast. Over Belgium and Germany somewhere the [enemy] fighters got right into the bomber stream and wrought havoc: aircraft going down – right, left and centre – behind us. There were so many that we stopped reporting them – we didn't want to upset Ron the navigator. With all this slaughter going on the timing of the variable zero hour became more important. And so we felt it vital to get an accurate fix on the 'Y Box', which meant flying straight and level for a while. It was while doing the straight and level that the flak got us. We had seen the ground-level flashes of flak, but if we had taken evasive action the all-important fix would be lost.

They got us the first salvo; damn good shooting! The control rods were divided, target indicators were set ablaze around the 4,000 lb bomb, petrol tanks were holed and there was a great hole in the rear fuselage floor. Panic for a brief second and then the quiet voice, cool as a cucumber, over the intercom from our skipper (Johnny Nicholls, DFC): 'Nothing for it fellows. Bale out!' I just carried out my parachute drill as practised – there was no time for clear thought. Seconds, quite a lot of seconds, after leaving the aircraft blew up. A bit too close for comfort! The parachute drill worked a treat and when the parachute opened I felt that I had been kicked by a mule from underneath! I corrected the swing. Then the earth came rushing up. I prepared to land as instructed, but a local updraught got me swinging again and I went the wrong way and cracked my ankle.

On landing I released the parachute and it collapsed. I gathered it up, kissing it and blessing all the 'parachute packing girls'. I buried the parachute in a snow drift and made my way to a wood. The moon was still high. I slipped on my broken ankle on some ice and fell. Further walking was impossible. I slithered off the ice, took out my flotation packs from my Irvin suit, put them under my hip and shoulder and then curled up and went to sleep. It was after midnight. I woke up at dawn when I could see my way to crawl into the wood. I took stock. There was a railway down to the roadway, so I decided to make my way down, using a stick to help myself. I was seen by a youth who came up and saluted me. I returned the salute and with his assistance made my way down to the road. He stopped a truck. I got into the cab and was taken to the local police station at Hachenberg.

The local schoolmaster was brought in to interrogate me. When he had finished telling me that I was a 'terror flyer' who killed women and children I replied: 'I remember in 1940 and 1941 when you bombed our churches!' I was kept standing up for my sins for a long time. Later that day I was taken to Dulag Luft[44] at Oberusel for Luftwaffe interrogation. I had the usual four days of solitary confinement with all the usual routines – shouting in my face, talking under the floor, etc. Then a bright, clever intelligence Obergefreiter had a 'go'. Having been well briefed I survived that without difficulty, as I did with the officer the following day. I was taken from the cells and sent to Hohemark Hospital, then on to Obermassfeld Hospital and on to Muningen Hospital for physiotherapy. Then on to Stalag Luft VII at Bankau for the summer and winter, and a winter march in front of the Russians to Luckenwalde. Then the Russians released us but continued to keep hold of us. Their bureaucracy was awful – nothing went right. Eventually a truck to the River Elbe, a plane to Brussels and a Lanc. bomber home.

Flight engineer and bomb-aimer Patrick Nolan was the only survivor when his plane was shot down on the way to bomb Kiel on 26 August 1944.

*Sgt Pat Nolan, 635 Squadron*: We were hit from astern by a nightfighter. My survival was a fluke. I was ejected through the hatch still attached to the aircraft systems. I was captured in Denmark about a week later.

Nolan too was imprisoned in Stalag Luft VII at Bankau and took part in the horrific march across the frozen wastelands to Luckenwalde.

The long, nightmarish winter march from Stalag Luft VII in Silesia to Stalag Luft IIIA at Luckenwalde, near Berlin, took place during late January and early February 1945 at the time of the Red Army's renewed offensive in Poland. For months the Russians had been held up outside Warsaw. Then suddenly the Red Army began their new offensive on the Vistula front and within a few days they had advanced right up to the Silesian border of Germany. As each prisoner-of-war camp became threatened by the advancing Russians the Germans evacuated them and forced the prisoners to march westwards. At the same time millions of civilians began walking, or riding on ox-carts, in appalling weather conditions in a great trek ahead of the Russians.

The camp at Stalag Luft VII where Nolan, Ogilvie and hundreds of other airmen were prisoners was evacuated on 19 January. During the airmen's 250 mile march it snowed frequently and there were blizzards; on one terrible night the temperature fell twenty degrees below freezing. Cold drinks turned to blocks of ice before they could be drunk and clothing became coated with snow and froze solid. Frostbite became increasingly common amongst both the prisoners and their guards. When the airmen eventually arrived at Luckenwalde they found a hopeless situation. The camp was already overcrowded with about 16,000 prisoners from many countries and conditions in the camp were absolutely deplorable. At that stage of the war the Germans were simply unable to provide adequate rations even if they had wanted to and as a result prisoners slowly starved to death. On 21 April the German guards unexpectedly disappeared. They were soon replaced, however, by Russian soldiers who, while generally very friendly, were hopelessly disorganized. It was not until 20 May – some twelve days after the war in Europe had officially finished – that a convoy of Russian lorries was at last made available to take prisoners further west. By then many of the prisoners, deciding that they had had enough and were not willing to wait, had already escaped and had left on foot.[45]

Another would-be escaper whose luck ran out was Donald Courtenay of 635 Squadron. Courtenay was the pilot and sole survivor of a Lancaster which had been attacked on 22 April 1944 by a German fighter over north-eastern France (see page 89). After parachuting he was injured on landing and was unable to move from where he lay. Fortunately, he was found the next day by a farm labourer and taken to a farm where he was given food and clothes. The following day Courtenay was taken to Paris, given some medical attention and hidden again for a month. On 25 May Courtenay was taken, along with nine other evaders, by members of the local underground organization on a 500 mile train journey to Pau, near the foot of the Pyrenees in the south-western corner of France. There they met a group of twenty-nine escaping Jews in a large barn outside the town. Afterwards all thirty-nine escapers left together and proceeded south to climb the pass over the mountains and attempt the crossing of the Spanish frontier thirty miles away.

*F/Lt Donald H. Courtenay, 635 Squadron*: On 2 June we commenced our attempt, led by professional guides. The airmen in the party had no food and as none was provided we became very exhausted. On 4 June the guide left us and, through straggling, our party was reduced to eighteen, including the six airmen. On 5 June, about two kilometres from the Spanish village of Isaba, four of our party, including myself, were cut off and captured by two German guards. We were then taken back to a small frontier town, searched and given a perfunctory interrogation, to which we did not reply. We spent the night in a cell in a private house. On 6 June we returned to Pau, and from there we were sent to St Michael Prison at Toulouse.[46]

Courtenay remained in prison for more than two months until 19 August when the Germans evacuated Toulouse and the prisoners were liberated by the Free French.

Successful evasions, especially during the middle years of the war, were comparatively rare and without the courageous and resourceful help of friendly civilians willing to risk their own lives there would probably have been none at all. But how was it possible to discern who was friendly and who was not? It was not easy to know, and many airmen walked around for days or hid in the woods for as long as possible before finally summoning up the nerve to ask for help.

Leonard Canning of 218 Squadron was fortunate when at last he found a farmer to help him. That was after he had been walking across eastern France for nearly a week. Canning was the engineer of X-Xray and had baled out in the dark after his plane had been shot down over Sedan

*Crew of E-Easy, 623 Squadron, with their Stirling in the background, 1943.* Steve C. Smith

on 16 April 1943. He landed in a tree and after extricating himself and climbing down he walked eastwards for an hour before meeting another crew member, wireless operator W. Hamilton. Together they decided to make for Spain and set out walking south along the banks of the Meuse.

When they reached Lerouville, six days and seventy miles later, Canning and Hamilton met a farmer who took them to his home and generously put them up for a couple of nights. Then a friend of the farmer took them on by train to Dole. After staying the night in a hotel in Dole they were taken early next morning to Frasne and then left to find their own way to the Swiss border twelve miles away. They asked a farmer they met on the way to direct them to the frontier, but he turned out to be drunk so they spent the rest of the day aimlessly wandering around, looking for some kind of clue to indicate the way they should take. Luckily, they met another helpful farmer who not only gave them directions for crossing the border but also put them up for the night. They crossed into Switzerland the following morning but were almost arrested by the Swiss police who sent them on to the capital Berne where they were interned for the next sixteen months. Eventually, in August 1944, Canning was able to leave Switzerland with a small group of evaders and after an eight-hour climb across the Alps they reached France again and the comparative safety of a Maquis stronghold. They were then taken to Thonon on the south bank of Lake Geneva and from there guided by members of the Maquis to Grenoble where contact was made with American troops coming up from the south.

Two members of 218 Squadron did, in fact, make it to Spain. James Paterson was the navigator of H-Harry when it was attacked by a fighter in bright moonlight on 16 August 1943 while on its way to bomb Turin. The Stirling caught fire and although the crew fought to put the fire out it soon, after a few minutes, became too fierce and they were forced to abandon the attempt. Only Paterson and rear-gunner McKinnon were able to escape from the blazing bomber. McKinnon was wounded and became a prisoner-of-war. Paterson managed to parachute into a field north of Lyons and, after burying his parachute and Mae-west in a wood, started walking towards Switzerland. Soon he came to the main road but he couldn't cross it openly as there was an alert on; indeed, the German fighter which had shot him down was still circling around, probably trying to indicate to personnel on the ground where he had landed. Paterson tried to stay out of sight, but this was difficult as two French women came up and stood talking to one another near where he was crouching.

*Sgt James L. Paterson, 218 Squadron*: The two women remained talking and, as I felt that the plane which was circling round and round was trying to indicate my whereabouts to the Germans, I had no option but to make my presence known to them. They tried to convince me that I would not get very far in uniform and suggested that I should remain where I was, saying that they would send me clothes and help. I agreed and went back into the wood. In about half-an-hour one of the women returned with another woman who brought some civilian clothes. I changed in the wood and walked out with them. They instructed me to take the arm of one of them, as if we were husband and wife, and we entered Amberieu. One of the women was in charge of an establishment here which appeared to be empty at the time, and I was put into a bed. On the [following] morning the lady explained that I would not be able to remain there, owing to the impossibility of feeding me. In the afternoon I was taken, disguised as a gardener (with a big hat, hoe and wheel-barrow) to another house.[47]

From there Paterson was helped by the Resistance to get to Spain.

The second airman who managed to get to Spain was Gerald Lorne who was in the same plane as Ian Robb (see page 94) when it was shot down on 30 August 1943. After jumping out Lorne had his foot broken when it was hit by flying wreckage from the plane as it blew up. The pain caused Lorne to lose consciousness when he landed and he lay on the ground for seven and a half hours, all the time with his parachute still caught up in the branches of a nearby tree. On regaining consciousness he retrieved the parachute, hid it and then staggered 500 yards to a farmhouse. At first Lorne wasn't sure whether he was in Germany or Holland, but then an old lady came out of the farmhouse, saw him and went back to fetch her husband. The two old people hid Lorne in a chicken-run and gave him food and coffee. Later they put him in a wheel-barrow and took him to a wood behind the farm where he lay in hiding for four days until the farmer was able to arrange for a grateful Lorne to travel incognito to Spain.

One 218 Squadron pilot that tried to escape from Germany itself was a New Zealander named Hyde. According to Bill Jackson, in *Three Stripes and Four Brownings*, Hyde had been shot down and had become a prisoner. 'However, he made a bid for freedom by attempting to steal a German aircraft. He all but got it off the ground but was recaptured and sent back to the prisoner-of-war camp.'[48]

By the time that 635 Squadron had formed at Downham Market the nature of the problem for crews forced down over enemy territory had changed. The allied invasion of northern France took place just over two months after the squadron had settled in at Downham and now the critical task confronting evading airmen was not so much escaping to a neutral country as staying hidden and waiting until overtaken by the allied forces. Sometimes it was a longish wait.

Philip Tweedy was the engineer of a 635 Squadron Lancaster when it took off on 20 May 1944, a couple of weeks before D-Day, to bomb Duisberg. On the return flight the plane was hit by flak and the pilot ordered his crew to abandon the aircraft. Tweedy baled out over Eindhoven in Holland. When he landed he found that he had lost both his boots and he had to improvise some footwear by cutting up his parachute and tying pieces over his feet. With bandaged feet he started to walk in the general direction of Belgium. After a while Tweedy came across a farmer who recognized his uniform and hid him in a field until he could find more help. The following day the farmer's friend put him up for a night and then he was moved on to a succession of different farms and houses, each one a little further west and thus nearer the allied lines. Eventually Tweedy and another airman were taken to a house in Brussels where they waited for the British troops to arrive in the capital on 3 September.

Squadron Leader H.M. Johnston's precarious return flight in a blazing Lancaster on 11/12 June 1944 has already been mentioned (see page 63). Of the four crew who baled out of the stricken plane over Nantes two of them, bomb-aimer R.A. Boddington and engineer J. Harrowing, managed to evade capture. Their journeys back to the allied lines turned out to be continual hide-and-seek contests as they were moved from place to place always one step ahead of the enemy.

*F/Lt R.A. Boddington, DFC, 635 Squadron*: [After] the rear-gunner reported the aircraft on fire, I grabbed the fire extinguisher, but on looking back, saw the aircraft was burning fiercely amidships. The pilot ordered us to abandon the aircraft. I jumped after the flight engineer at 1500 feet, my parachute opening immediately. I landed unhurt on soft ground in a vineyard and buried my parachute and Mae West.[49]

Boddington then started walking away from the vineyard. Almost right away he found himself at the edge of a Luftwaffe airfield so he turned back and walked in the opposite direction. He was going along a bridle path when two German soldiers suddenly appeared from behind a hedge.

*F/Lt R.A. Boddington, DFC*: I actually knocked into one of them. I said 'Bonjour Monsieur', stopped for a moment as if I had lost my way and turned back, retracing my steps down the path. A youth on a cycle passed me slowly and said 'Anglais?' and I said 'Oui.' He said 'Vite – vite Allemands.' I kept my pace, however, until I had gone six hundred yards when I heard firing and bullets whistled past me. I then started to run and almost immediately came to a turning which screened me from the guards; looking round I saw that they were searching for me and shouting. I got behind a hedge and continued running for about two miles, before I came to a farmhouse. I looked around this farm to see if any Germans were billeted there and crossed the farmyard and sat down on the other side, waiting for the French people near the barn to approach me. This they did, pointed to my uniform and asked 'Anglais?' When I said 'Yes' they assured me by their gestures that I was among friends. They gave me coffee and also dressed me in civilian clothes.[50]

From then on Boddington's journey was arranged for him. After first being taken to stay in a house in Nantes on the opposite side of the Loire he was moved to a house in the village of Haute Indre for three days and then taken by boat twelve miles down river to La Belle Ile where he spent five days in a cow-byre.

Meanwhile Harrowing had made contact with members of the Maquis and was staying with a group of them in a wood near Lyon d'Or twenty miles south of Nantes. On 21 June Boddington was taken back up river again in a rowing boat to Haute Indre and then by cycle to join Harrowing at the Maquis camp. After a couple of days the camp was struck and Boddington and Harrowing were given instructions to cycle to Le Pellerin on the south bank of the Loire.

Here they stayed the night with a family whose two daughters made a habit, after each allied raid, of cycling around the countryside looking for airmen who might be hiding in the vicinity. The following day Boddington and Harrowing went back to La Belle Ile where they met up again with their navigator E. Warmington and two American airmen who had been discovered by the two Pellerin girls. The five airmen were then ferried across to the north bank of the river and driven, with a load of pigs in a covered truck, to another Maquis camp twenty-one miles north of Nantes, near Saffre.

The Saffre camp was a large one with over three hundred partisans housed in two farmhouses and outbuildings and was guarded by sentries. A few days after the airmen arrived the camp was attacked by the Germans and in the confusion which followed the five airmen attempted to escape. When they tried to cross a road the Germans opened fire and the airmen scattered. Harrowing and one of the American airmen disappeared into the undergrowth and remained hidden there for three days before retracing their steps back to Le Pellerin. Boddington, Warmington and the other American tried to cross the road a second time but the Germans were ready and only Boddington managed to escape when they opened fire again.

Boddington returned to the wood and while hiding there heard what he thought was a tracker-dog stumbling about the undergrowth searching for him; in fact, this proved to be a wild boar dashing past. In the afternoon, after things had quietened down a bit, he started out again on his own and eventually came to a farm near a reservoir close to the Forest of Vioreau where he was told that he could stay and rest as long as he liked. Apart from one further scare when he had to hide in a wood, Boddington stayed at the farm for more than five weeks. Then on 5 August, after hearing on the radio that American troops had reached Rennes, he left the farm and, despite the fact that German soldiers were still encamped on the opposite side of the reservoir, cycled north towards the allied lines. Boddington got as far as Chateaubriant and found, to his delight, that the Germans had just left, leaving the town to be held lightly by one American captain and thirty men.

Harrowing, who had left Boddington in the forest near Saffre, arrived at Le Pellerin again on 4 July. He stayed at Le Pellerin and on La Belle Ile for seven weeks until the Americans had reached the north bank of the Loire and had captured Nantes. On 22 August Harrowing rowed across the Loire and made his way into Nantes to make contact with the Americans.

At least six other airmen from 635 Squadron managed to parachute into France and escape capture during the last few months of hostilities. William Shepherd and Michael Haberlin were two survivors of a Lancaster which crashed at Beaurains, near Arras, on 15 June 1944. Bomb-aimer Shepherd baled out over Lens and was immediately taken to a farm where he remained in hiding until British tanks passed the farm on 5 September. Navigator Haberlin broke his foot on landing just fifty yards from the burning wreck of his plane. A local woman bound his foot in a splint and then, after lying in a field for a day and in a garden shed for a further three days, he was moved to a safe house in Arras where a doctor put his foot in plaster. Haberlin stayed on in Arras until he was able to make contact with Allied troops on 1 September.

Douglas Cameron, G. Goddard, Charles Godfrey, and G.R. Turner were all part of the crew of Ian Bazalgette's Lancaster which crashed at Senantes on 4 August 1944 (see page 91). All four managed to parachute out at only a thousand feet and were hidden by villagers in local farms and houses. The rear-gunner Cameron had a narrow escape. After being rescued by two French officers the building where they were staying and transmitting radio messages was taken over by the Germans for their wounded. Cameron and the French men hid under the bed with their equipment for three hours before they were able to get away. Navigator Goddard and wireless operator Godfrey were hidden the first night in the local gendarme's house and then taken by horse and cart to a farm in the next village. Later, after SS troops started going to the

*S/Ldr I.W. Bazalgette and crew, 635 Squadron, 1944. The pilot S/Ldr Bazalgette, VC (far left) and the bomb-aimer F/Lt I. Hibbert, DFC (2nd from left) were killed when their Lancaster was shot down by flak over France on 4 August 1944. F/O D. Cameron, DFM (1st from right), F/Lt G. Goddard (1st from left), F/O C. Godfrey, DFC (centre) and Sgt G. Turner (far right) parachuted from the stricken bomber and were each rescued and hidden by local villagers.* C. Godfrey

farm to get produce, they were moved to a camp in a forest near Beauvais where they stayed in hiding with another British airman and some American airmen. Every evening at dusk villagers took them food until they were liberated by British troops on 30 August. Turner, the flight engineer, hurt his back when baling out. He was fortunate, however, to be found immediately by a member of the French Resistance and was hidden on a farm until liberated.

In northern Holland the war was still a long way from being over on 5 January 1945 when navigator William Douglas and rear-gunner Arthur Clayton baled out of their Lancaster near Groningen. After landing close to the German border Douglas hid his gear in a ditch and walked westwards for about ten hours before contacting a farmer in Stadskanaal who hid him at his farm. Douglas was fortunate to be able to stay throughout the period of his evasion at the same farm until Canadian troops arrived on 15 April. Clayton's evasion was less straight-forward. He was moved back and forth between six different houses and farms before being eventually taken to stay at an asylum.

*W/O Arthur D. Clayton, 635 Squadron*: One evening I was taken to a shoe-maker living in the local asylum, which was almost a town of its own. I stayed with [him] until 20 February. I was there for about three nights and then taken to the Director of the asylum and slept in his strong room in the offices. The next afternoon, a nurse and a member of the underground arrived with three cycles. They took papers off the Director certifying that I was mentally deficient as well as deaf and dumb. They took me back to Veendam by cycle to the Town Hall. I stayed with the caretaker from that date until 15 April. A butcher in the town supplied me with food during my stay. I was liberated by [the] Polish Tank Division.[51]

By April 1945 even airmen who came down in Germany itself stood a chance of evading the enemy. George Wilson was returning from a bombing raid on Harburg when his Lancaster was shot down by a German fighter. He baled out and landed in a marsh near Meppen, not far from the Dutch border.

*P/O George Wilson, 635 Squadron*: It took me about three hours to extricate myself, after which I rested in a wood until dawn. I then started to walk and reached a small village called

## INSTRUCTIONS

(1) Learn by heart the Russian phrase "Ya Anglicháhnin" (*means "I am English" and is pronounced as spelt*).

(2) Carry this folder and contents in left breast pocket.

(3) If you have time before contact with Russian troops, take out the folder and attach it (*flag side outwards*) to front of pocket.

(4) When spotted by Russian troops put up your hands holding the flag in one of them and call out the phrase "Ya Anglicháhnin."

(5) If you are spotted before taking action as at para 3 do **NOT** attempt to extract folder or flag. Put up your hands and call out phrase "Ya Anglicháhnin". The folder will be found when you are searched.

(6) You must understand that these recognition aids **CANNOT** be accepted by Soviet troops as proof of bona fides as they may be copied by the enemy. They should however protect you until you are cross questioned by competent officers.

# Я англичанин

"**Ya Anglicháhnin**" (*Pronounced as spelt*)

Пожалуйста сообщите сведения обо мне в Британскую Военную Миссию в Москве

Please communicate my particulars to British Military Mission Moscow.

*The leaflet issued to Mosquito crews who landed in Russian-held territory.* Dr B.J. Sherry

Adorf. I was approached by a man who, although obviously a German, said 'Kamerad'. He gave me food and told me roughly where the British troops were. He and another man then borrowed two bicycles and took me to a little place near Nordorn where I made contact with our own Household Cavalry.[52]

608 Squadron suffered remarkably few losses over enemy territory and consequently its evaders were few in number. Throughout the first four months of 1945 the squadron continued with its intensive series of long-distance bombing raids to Berlin. Now, as the Russians approached ever nearer to Berlin the Mosquito crews flying from Downham had the choice – if they were badly shot up over the 'Big City' – of either trying to make a dash for home or continuing to fly eastwards and parachuting in to Russian-occupied territory. Should they choose the latter they had already been taught to say 'Ya Anglichahnin' ('I am English'). To help in identification they were also issued with little silk Union Jacks on the back of which was a message printed in Russian which said: 'Please communicate my particulars to British Military Mission Moscow.'

A notable evader – indeed, one who became something of a legend amongst 608 Squadron crews – was Flying Officer Harry Tyrrell, or 'Harry the Dutchman' as he was affectionately known. His real name, in fact, was Harry Hoyt. Tyrrell was a *nom de guerre* to cover his real identity in case he was shot down. His navigator was Sergeant Esban, a refugee from Czechoslovakia. At the beginning of the war Tyrrell had been a pilot with the Dutch Air Force but was shot down by the Germans. After the occupation of Holland he joined the Dutch Resistance until he was sent to a labour camp by the Germans and forced to work on the railways.

Somehow he escaped from the camp and managed to make his way to Britain despite an injured foot which gave him a limp.

The injury did not, however, affect his flying and soon he joined the RAF. Tyrrell had been flying with 608 Squadron for some time when, towards the end of February 1945, his Mosquito was shot down over Magdeburg while returning from a Berlin raid. Tyrrell was picked up by the Germans and interrogated, but, despite his thick English accent, was not recognized. Then, in the confusion surrounding the German retreat, he not only succeeded in escaping from the Germans a second time but also managed, while on the run, to call in to see his family in Holland. In April he was reported to be back in London. When later Harry revisited Downham a delighted squadron threw an informal party in his honour and, so the story goes, most of the champagne that had been carefully conserved for expected end-of-the-war festivities was drunk in the course of the impromptu celebrations.

## CHAPTER 10

# The Final Fling

As the war drew to its relentless climax the frequency of operations was stepped up. In September 1944 the combined number of sorties carried out by both Pathfinder squadrons was over three hundred for that month alone. By March 1945 the monthly total of sorties flown by 608 and 635 Squadrons was almost five hundred. It was during this frenetic period that records began to be broken and a number of individual airmen completed a hundred or more operational sorties.

The first to complete a hundred sorties was Squadron Leader Jimmy Dow, DSO, DFC, of the Royal Canadian Air Force. Dow was a bomb-aimer with 635 Squadron and notched up his 'century' on 30 October 1944 on a raid to Cologne. He was soon followed by Wing Commander Dennis Witt, DSO, DFC. Witt had already completed sixty-five sorties with 7 and 10 Squadrons when he was appointed to the headquarters of 8 (Pathfinder) Group in August 1943. He then managed to get himself put back on operations and was posted to 635 Squadron as its flight commander. He soon became a Master Bomber and completed his hundredth sortie with a raid on Duisberg on 30 November 1944. Wing Commander S. 'Tubby' Baker, DSO, DFC, had also served with 7 Squadron before being posted to Downham Market. In September 1944 he took over as 635 Squadron's commanding officer but still continued to take part in operations. He made his 'century' on 13 March 1945 while acting as Master Bomber on a raid to Wuppertal. Two days later Baker relinquished his post as commanding officer and left 635 Squadron.

608 Squadron also had a couple of 'centuries'. They were achieved by Wing Commander R.C. Alabaster, DSO, DFC, and Flight Lieutenant Cook, DFC, DFM. Alabaster's 'century' was a mixed bag for he had completed his first two tours of duty as a navigator and it was not until January 1944 that he qualified as a pilot. In November 1944 he became 608 Squadron's commanding officer.

March 1945 was the busiest month in the airfield's short history and operations were carried out on every night except one. 635 Squadron's Lancasters took part in seventeen raids. These still included Cologne, Hamburg and targets in the Ruhr, and further afield Nuremberg and Chemnitz. The Mosquitos of 608 Squadron took part in forty raids including no fewer than twenty-eight to the German capital Berlin.

In April there was a slight slackening in the tempo but no lessening of its fury. One important raid executed during the earlier part of the month was on the Deutsche Werke U-boat yards at Kiel on 9 April. For 635 Squadron the high-point of the operation was the sinking of the German pocket-battleship *Admiral Scheer* by one of its Lancasters, piloted by Flight Lieutenant Parkes, DFC. His 'blind' bomb-aimer, Flight Sergeant McCallum, was later awarded the Distinguished Flying Medal for his part in the action.

During April, the last full month of the war in Europe, many of the raids carried out from Downham were slightly unusual in that they were often the last raid of a particular city. Leipzig was bombed for the last time on the 10th, Nuremberg on the 11th, Hamburg on the 13th, Berlin on the 20th, Bremen on the 22nd, and Munich on the 25th April. The last raid to Berlin had been 608 Squadron's eighty-seventh raid on the capital. The following day, 21 April, 608 Squadron sent twelve Mosquitos to attack Kiel. Unfortunately one aircraft was shot down; this was the last of Downham's planes which failed to return from operations.

*Sergeant's Mess party, 635 Squadron.* P. Cronin, via P. Dascombe

The last two operations in which 635 Squadron took part were both on 25 April. In the first raid, an early morning operation to Berchtesgaden, 635 Squadron's fifteen Lancasters were part of a massive force of 375 aircraft for which the Master Bomber was the squadron's own commanding officer Wing Commander J. Fordham. This raid to Hitler's 'Eagle's Nest' hideout high up in the Bavarian Alps was more of a symbolic gesture than part of a battle for a military objective. Hitler himself was in Berlin at the time.

*F/Lt L.J. Melling, DFC, 635 Squadron*: On my very last trip we took off before dawn and one of my strongest memories is the exhilarating sight of the Alps as we flew over in the clear early morning with the sun shining on the snowy peaks.[53]

Over Berchtesgaden itself the weather was different and snow and mist made it difficult to identify any precise targets.

*F/Sgt Wally H. Hitchcock, DFM, 635 Squadron*: I remember the Berchtesgaden trip quite well. According to my Log Book we left Downham at 5.39 am. The flight was uneventful to the target. Over the target, which could not be seen clearly due to the concentration of bombs bursting and debris being thrown into the air, the flak was slight. There was no fighter opposition.

The raid was, nevertheless, successful and the Berghof, where Hitler had previously held his conferences, the SS barracks and houses belonging to Bormann and Goering were all demolished. One Lancaster, unable to unload its bombs over the target, dropped them over Prien instead.

The second raid of the day took place in the afternoon and was to the Wangerooge coastal batteries on the Frisian Islands. Again 635 Squadron's four Lancasters were part of a larger

*A guard of honour from RAF Marham stands to attention outside Bexwell church in May 1983 at the unveiling of the memorial to Arthur Aaron and Ian Bazalgette, both of whom won the Victoria Cross while flying on operations from RAF Downham Market.* West Norfolk Newspapers Ltd

force. Bombing out of a clear sky the raid caused much damage to the surroundings of the gun batteries but little harm to the guns themselves. By 7 pm that evening all of 635 Squadron's Lancasters had returned for the last time and landed at Downham.

On the evening of the 25th some of the crews of 635 Squadron celebrated what was to be for them the end of hostilities.

**F/Sgt Wally H. Hitchcock, DFM**: We gathered with our groundcrews, who always did a marvellous job on our aircraft, at the Crown pub for a last session. All I can remember about that was attempting to return to the camp after dark on my bike and riding straight into a brick wall, which did neither myself or the front wheel any good.

For the crews of 608 Squadron there were still three more operations to carry out. The first, on the night of 25/26 April, involved twelve Mosquitos dropping leaflets over prisoner-of-war camps in Germany. On the following night another twelve Mosquitos raided Eggebek airfield in Schleswig-Holstein. There was no opposition, but one plane had to make an emergency landing at Woodbridge airfield on its return.

608 Squadron's last raid and, indeed, the RAF's final raid of the European air-war came on 2/3 May when, fearing that the Germans were assembling ships at Kiel to transport troops to Norway, an attack was ordered on the port. A hundred and twenty-six Mosquitos attacked in two waves, an hour apart. Eight Mosquitos, carrying 4,000 lb bombs, from 608 Squadron participated in each wave. The last Mosquito took off from Downham an hour before midnight

and by 2.18 am had returned safely to base. It was the very last RAF bomber to drop a bomb in anger in Europe.

The war was not, however, yet quite over. There were still errands of mercy to be performed. In fact, a large part of Holland was still occupied by German forces and, in order to feed the starving civilian population, a truce was arranged to allow food to be dropped. This was officially known as Operation Manna, but to the aircrews the missions were known as 'Spam raids'. From 30 April to 8 May Lancasters of 635 Squadron took part in the Operation by marking out dropping zones near The Hague and Rotterdam so that food supplies could be parachuted in.

On Monday 7 May Germany finally surrendered unconditionally. The war in Europe was over at last and people could breathe freely once more. By dusk that evening spontaneous celebrations had begun and Downham's Market Square was soon heaving as a large crowd gathered to let off steam by singing and dancing. The thronging mass naturally included many airmen and WAAFs from the airfield as well as some British and American soldiers. Street lights were turned on in the town for the first time since the Blackout and over Bexwell Aerodrome two searchlights formed a victory 'V' in the sky. Down in the Market Square an Australian airman made an abortive attempt to climb up the cast-iron clock tower. From somewhere a ladder was quickly found and with this the airman tried once again to scale the Town Clock. This time he was successful. He reached the minute hand, pulled it back to half-past ten and then, to the roaring acclaim of the crowd below, draped a bright blue pair of WAAF knickers over it.

VE (Victory in Europe) Day was officially observed the following day, 8 May. On the airfield festivities started with a station parade.

*F/Lt Harry S.T. Harris, DFC, 608 Squadron*: Not only was the band suffering the effects of too much alcohol the night before but everyone around me had similar symptoms. We were all glad it was a short affair and immediately afterwards Tony and self set out to celebrate. I was on my bike with Tony on the cross-bar and speeding down the hill to the railway station when there was a loud clanging of a bell and a police car drew in front of us. Apparently it was illegal to carry a passenger on a bike in this manner, but we only got a slight reprimand and went on our way to the station with Tony riding in the police car.

Many left the camp temporarily to enjoy themselves, but for those who stayed celebrations continued in one of the large aircraft hangars.

In Downham Market and the surrounding villages thanksgiving services were held in the various churches and chapels and flags and bunting flew from houses everywhere. At dusk the revelry of the previous night was repeated and another large crowd gathered in the Market Square to celebrate. Coloured lights appeared almost miraculously on buildings and numerous bonfires were lit in Downham's park and waste spaces and in the grounds of many country estates. In the Market Square the crowd danced to the music of a professional band. An extension of licensing hours was granted up until 11 pm, but before that time had been reached many pubs and hotels had already run dry, such was the demand on a limited supply.

On the airfield at Downham there was a stand-down for about a week after VE Day. According to some wags it had been arranged to allow sufficient time for the aircrews to recover from their celebrations! Then flying continued with Operation Exodus. This involved flying to airfields in Germany and Belgium to pick up British ex-prisoners-of-war who had recently been liberated from the prison camps. 635 Squadron had already contributed to Operation Exodus when on 7 May eleven of its Lancasters had ferried 243 ex-prisoners home from Brussels. On 11 May the squadron sent planes to Lubeck in Germany to collect more ex-

## 's' Work
## 'wnham

...ber, members of W.V.S. and their been knitting gar- dren of the liber- and to date have sent away 285

...ith, deputy W.V.S. Downham Market, ...f these activities, ...ceived the follow- ...om Mrs Cranage, ...ry, Norwich, the y organiser:

...ks for the two ...woollies received They are really a ...ll your knitters e are to them for hey are doing for

...still goes on, and ...nents are display- ...shop-window lent Wright.

## Between
## ...ends

he news was pub- "Lynn News and ...t Mrs. Titford, of ...n. Downham West, a card from her hear, in Malaya ...and her husband

...s. Titford received ...rs. Molly Tatham, ...', Western Aus- ...hat she had read ...in the "Lynn ...rtiser," which is regularly by Lynn expressing ' her ...arning that the she knew when ...laya, were alive

...t says she lived ...r nine years at ...rv...he Techni- ...f...eet Sugar ...son of the Rev. P. ...rector of Great Fakenham, was a ...of the F.M.S. ...'s. He returned 18½ days of his long leave in ...lia to report to his Lumpur and was ...1942, while man- ...un.

...concludes her let- ...lovely to know Mrs. Phear were that I felt I just ...you."

## Exam List
## ...ttisham

...nettisham Metho- ...chool, who passed ...amination were: ...l Sadler; first- ...t Drysdale, Ann y Holmes, Sheila ...llis Mansbridge, ...', Margaret Rand, ...nettisham school ...or the Bennett

# VE-DAY at DOWNHAM

# Thanksgiving Services
# And Open - Air
# Rejoicing

Unofficial spontaneous celebra- tions began in Downham at dusk on Monday. A large crowd gathered 'n the Market-place and there was impromptu dancing to bugle music provided by some lads of the A.T.C. band who had earlier been on a parade.

The crowd included many air- men and W.A.A.F.S. from Down- ham R.A.F. station whose exist- ence may now be publicly men- tioned) as well as British and American troops and a repre- sentative or two of the Senior Service.

From the roof of an Army truck cheers for Churchill, Truman and Stalin were called for and enthusiastically given, and there was another cheer when hun- dreds of coloured lights on the "Castle" Hotel were switched on.

Breaking into song, the crowd gave enthusiastic if not too musi- cal renderings of "Roll out the barrel," "Rule Britannia" and "Land of Hope and Glory" and all joined hands for "Auld Lang Syne."

### DRAPERY

One Australian airman made unsuccessful attempts to climb the town clock. Not to be de- terred, he foraged out a ladder and at imminent risk of becom- ing airborne he managed to reach the minute hand of the south face which was pointing to quar- ter-to-eleven. He pulled it back to 10.30, draped it with a bright blue lady's garment which is not usually displayed in public, and returned the hand to the quarter- to position. Rising to the oc- casion, the clock ignored its rough handling and continued to tick out the minutes with the banner hanging to the minute- hand! Later, it revolted and time stood still.

### CELESTIAL V

Street lights were turned on for an hour and the front of the Howdale Home was well illumin- ated. Two searchlights on the aerodrome maintained a "V" in the sky over Downham.

On VE-Day morning everyone was busy putting up flags and bunting and soon the streets and roads were gay with colour.

### CHURCH SERVICES

There was large attendances at services of thanksgiving at church and chapel. At St. Ed- mund's parish church, services were held at 8, 11 and 6.30, and there were united Free Church services at the London-rd. Metho- dist church at 10.45 and in the evening. Special services were also held at St. Dominic's Roman Catholic church and at the Sal.

world that had been overrun. If this 'country had fallen Downham Market would' have been under the heel of the Ger- mans and there was little doubt that the occurrences of the' other occupied countries would have had their counterpart in Down- ham.

### CASUALTIES

"When we think of what we have been spared we may well give thanks for God this afternoon for our deliverance." Another thing for which we could all be deeply grateful was the fact that, speaking generally, we had been delivered from the mass slaugh- ter of the last war. No-one knew what lay ahead in the Japanese war but hitherto casualties had not been so grievous as in the last war, and we might well say that Downham had been particularly blessed in that respect. The third great cause for gratitude was that Downham had been spared the horrors of bombing. The town had no scars and really had not had an incident. "So may we sharpen our gratitude to God by considerations like these," he concluded. "Praise the Lord oh my soul and all that is within me praise His holy Name."

Arrangements for the service were in the hands of a committee comprising Messrs. C. E. Bowman (chairman), H. Alflatt, R. B. Collins, J. Hinton, M. L. Hutson, E. A. Walker, J. T. Waterson and D. S. Hudson (secretary). Mr. H. Mann provided amplifying equipment.

### VICTORY PEALS

The bells of the parish church rang out Victory peals from 7.15 to 7.45 on Tuesday morning and again for an hour in the after- noon. There was more bell-ring- ing at night. Bob Triples and Bob Major were rung. The ringers were Malcolm Mastin (treble), Andrew Burbeck, E. Mastin (conductor), F. Farnham, S. G. Elsey, H. Burbeck, F. J. Elsey, jun., and F. J. Elsey (tenor). During the morning, the ringers went to Stow church, where there is a dearth of ringers, and rang for half-an-hour.

An extension of licensing hours until 11 p.m. was granted in Downham on VE-Day, but before that hour a number of licensees had run short of supplies.

### HITLER'S EFFIGY

When dusk fell, bonfires were lighted, notable one being at Re- treat Estate and in Mr. Raby's Paradise-rd. field. At the latter, fifty children gathered and cheer- ed when the effigy of Hitler was burnt. Fireworks saved from pre-war days were also enjoyed. A large crowd gathered on the

### WAR CHARITIES TALK AT TILNEY

The monthly meeting of Tilney St. Lawrence Women's Institute was held in the Oddfellows' hall on Wednesday, sixteen members being present. Miss M. Nelson (president) presided, supported by Mrs. H. Rush (vice-president), Miss Hall (treas.) and Miss D. Bennett (sec.).

A talk on the work of Norfolk War Charities was given by Miss Ruscoe (Norwich), who was thanked by Mrs. A. Fake. A "bring and buy" stall in aid of the Norfolk War Charities will be held at the next meeting.

Games were organised by Mrs. Clare and Mrs. Riches and were won by Mrs. Sanders and Mrs. Rennie. The monthly competi- tion was won by Mrs. Nelson, sen., for the best supper-dish. Mrs. K. Allen was in charge of teas.

### CANE-WORK AT MASSINGHAM

Massingham Women's Institute were disappointed not to have a demonstration on needle-weaving by Mrs. Hansen, secretary of the County handicrafts committee, at their May meeting, but enjoyed one on cane-work by Mrs. Rix, one of their vice-presidents, who is also a member of the handi- crafts committee.

Mrs. Rix presided over the meeting, and Miss Seaman judged a competition for home-made buttons, awarding highest marks to Miss King with Mrs. Howes second, and Mrs. G. H. Leverett third. It was announced that awards for the exhibits at the County exhibition averaged 90 per cent. Some 250 eggs sent to Gay- ton infirmary were contributed by members and friends. A miniature whist drive proved popular, and tea followed.

### PRISONER'S STORY AT TILNEY ALL SAINTS

The May meeting of Tilney All Saints Women's Institute was held in the Barn, Mrs. Nicholson presiding. Miss Reeve was re- sponsible for an effort entitled "A garland of flowers," in which sev- eral members took part, with Miss F. Baker as Queen of May. A competition for a bunch of red, white and blue flowers was won by Miss Reeve.

Mr. Tom Hearle, very recently returned from a P.O.W. camp in Germany, gave a talk on a prisoner's life and stressed how much the Red Cross parcels had meant to the men in keeping them fit and morale high. He was presented with cigarettes by the president, and thanked for his talk by Mrs. L. Reeve. Mrs. Shinn, Mrs. Patrick, and helpers served refreshments and the meeting closed with "The King."

**Women's Institute reports for which we cannot find room on Friday are published in Tuesday's "Lynn News and Ad- vertiser" and vice versa.**

*A newspaper report of the VE-Day celebrations at Downham Market in May 1945.* Lynn News & Advertiser

*Lancaster Z-Zebra of 635 Squadron at Lübeck, Germany, with British ex-prisoners-of-war on 11 May 1945.*
Imperial War Museum BU5892

prisoners. Later in the same month the aircraft were used to fly out RAF maintenance crews to Juvincourt in France and bring back still more ex-prisoners.

During the last week of May and throughout much of June small groups of aircraft were daily engaged in what was drolly referred to as 'Cooks' Tours'. These flights carried groundcrews over the war-damaged areas of northern Europe so that they were able to see for themselves the awful havoc which they had helped to wreak. Anyone on the station wanting to go on a trip in a Lancaster to 'see the sights' had to put his name down on a list and then wait for an available plane. Usually a couple of Lancasters – each carrying six passengers – flew out over Belgium or the Netherlands and then on to Germany and across the Rhineland, flying low so that the ruins of Cologne and the bomb-flattened cities of the Ruhr could be clearly seen.

*F/Lt Harry S.T. Harris, DFC*: On one occasion the Lancaster was being flown very low along the River Rhine when it hit a guard tower on a corner of a German prisoner-of-war camp. From the astro-dome I could see that a part of the starboard tail-fin had been torn off but the Lancaster was a tough bird and we got back to Downham. There it was judiciously taxied to behind the maintenance hangar and after some 'deliberations' the repairs were done without any enquiry.

The Mosquitos of 608 Squadron also participated in these peaceful missions across what had once been the mighty Reich, for many of the Mossie crews had only flown by night and so had never witnessed the terrible results of their own bombing. For all, whether groundcrew or aircrew, it was an unforgettable experience, but particularly so for those who had sat for the first time in a Lancaster's very restricted rear-gun turret for ten or more hours or for the occasional passenger wedged in the cramped nose of a Mosquito.

*Lancaster F-Freddie of 635 Squadron, also at Lübeck, with British ex-prisoners-of-war waiting to board the plane that will take them home, 11 May 1945.* Imperial War Museum BU5898

Gradually the spirit of the station changed. After the exhilarating and often very traumatic experience of participating in a long and devastating war there now came a mood of gloomy anti-climax. Some airmen who had been away from the airfield on leave over the VE Day period noticed changes when they returned for things began to settle down surprisingly soon into something like peace-time conditions.

**Cpl H.W.S. Gable, Motor Transport**: On my return the station had already altered considerably. There was a thinning out of personnel and parades, colour-hoisting, etc., were more on the lines of a pre-war station. Weekend passes could be had easily, so at weekends the camp was quite depleted.

F/Lt Alex Thorne, DSO, DFC, returning to the airfield three weeks after VE Day as a result of illness, remembered that 'an air of anti-climax pervaded throughout the station. The majority of aircrews had already dispersed, and Lancasters were being taken from their dispersal points and flown away to finish their lives in various ways, mostly on RAF Maintenance Units. The Messes were sparsely populated and among those who used them the main topics of conversation were centred upon the possibilities of when, and to where, the next batch of postings would determine their future until their demob dates.'[54]

For a while there was still a certain amount of activity. Some aircrews had volunteered to join 'Tiger Force' to carry on the fight in the Pacific against the Japanese and for this it was expected that 635 Squadron would re-equip with Avro Lincolns and then eventually fly out to a base on Okinawa. As a consequence cross-country flying and bombing and fighter affiliation exercises were still performed regularly. In addition the squadron was engaged in Operation

'Post Mortem' for a week at the end of June. The Operation involved flying to Flensburg, on the Danish/German border, and taking part in simulated attacks on German radar installations (manned by allied personnel) to evaluate the German early warning system.

On 6 August the first atomic bomb was dropped on Japan and just over a week later, on the 14th, Japan surrendered. The following day, Wednesday 15 August, was VJ (Victory over Japan) Day and a national holiday. At last the war was finished and really over. On the airfield at Downham a thanksgiving service was held in the morning in one of the hangars. After that the men and women had the remainder of the day off. Later in the month a Victory Tea was laid on in Downham Market for hundreds of local children. Among those who helped to serve, according to the local newspaper, were several airmen from the airfield and 'as one decorated Pathfinder aircrew member said: "We thoroughly enjoyed it and it gave us a chance to show our appreciation of all that the WVS canteen had done for us".'[55]

Then came the news that both squadrons at Downham were to be broken up. Despite the overwhelming joy of a world at peace at last, the decision to disband the squadrons was sad news for many people, both on and off the airfield, for countless numbers of friendships had been made between the airmen and airwomen at RAF Downham on the one hand and between the people on the airfield and the civilians living in Downham and the surrounding villages on the other hand. There followed a spate of smaller-scale celebrations as villages and pubs gave parties to honour the airmen who had been regular visitors to their communities and who had found friendship with the locals.

*Cpl H.W.S. Gable*: The landlord of the little pub by the river [at Stowbridge] asked me to bring the 'boys' over, if possible, before we finally left. I did this and, to our surprise, he had laid on a sausage-and-mash supper. The villagers came and we had a right royal evening.

*F/O B.J. Sherry, DFC, 608 Squadron*: I remember a great party being thrown for a bunch of us in the village hall [between Downham and Wisbech]. It was a great success . . . lashings of beer . . . lots of laughter and good cheer . . . marvellous food. Where the latter came from God only knows.

608 Squadron was the first unit to be disbanded. On 24 August all flying training ceased and four days later the last of the squadron's Mosquitos was delivered to RAF Upper Heyford for disposal.

635 Squadron continued for a little while longer. For much of August it took part in Operation Dodge and was engaged in transporting army personnel from Italy back to Britain. The last operation recorded in the Squadron Record Book was on 28 August: '2 aircraft detailed for Operation Dodge. 4 aircraft returned from Bari, each having transported 20 passengers which they landed at Tibbenham.' On 1 September 1945, one day before the official signing of Japan's surrender, 635 Squadron was disbanded.

Group Captain Cox, DSO, DFC, AFC, had already, on 31 August, relinquished command of the airfield and he moved to Transport Command. Almost the last thing that he did while stationed at Downham was to attend a 'Farewell Dance to the Squadrons' held in Downham's Town Hall. Here, in a poignant and nostalgic atmosphere, he expressed an appreciation for the welcome and hospitality which he said all RAF personnel had received from the community.

Soon the airfield had a forsaken look about it. The removal of the aircraft and the reduction in personnel had an immediate effect on Downham Market itself. As the local newspaper reported at the time: 'it has come as something of a shock on recent evenings to note the deserted appearance of Downham's streets. We have become so accustomed in recent years to having large numbers of service people about the streets, in the cinema, clubs, pubs and other public places

*The entrance to the site of the airfield in 1992. The building on the right-hand side housed the Guard Room and the Fire Party.*

that it will take a long time to get used to "normal" conditions. There is a very real feeling of regret in the town at the departure of so many whom we have come to regard as friends.'[56]

In October Downham Market was transferred from Bomber Command to Maintenance Command. It was intended to use the airfield to store aircraft, but this never, in fact, happened. Instead the airfield was transferred back to Bomber Command in December as a satellite of RAF Marham. Again nothing much happened and from May 1946 it was again put on a care and maintenance status. The airfield was finally closed on 24 October 1946 after just over four years' existence.

After the closure of the airfield most of the land on which it had been constructed reverted back to the original owners. Part of the land to the north of the A1122 road was sold to various manufacturing companies and part became a highway depot for Norfolk County Council and a depot for the Anglia Water Authority. The dormitory sites south of the road were used at first as a Land Army hostel between 1947 and 1949 before being taken over by the District Council and converted into civilian dwellings. Most of the dormitory huts and other buildings of the camp have been demolished. A few buildings still remain here and there, converted to other uses or abandoned.

The three concrete runways have all been laboriously dug up, much of the concrete being crushed to use as hardcore in the construction of the Downham Market by-pass on the A10. The by-road which once, before the building of the airfield, led from Crimplesham to Wimbotsham has been re-opened, but on a slightly different alignment. In fact, the by-road now follows, in part, a stretch of the concrete perimeter track which ran around the airfield joining up the ends of the runways. So much has changed, however, that it is difficult, when standing there, to look back and visualize the great four-engined bombers trundling their way along this section of the perimeter track in the dusk on their way to take-off positions on the main runway.

The countryside is at peace now. Long may it remain so. The plaque inside St Mary's church at Bexwell reminds us, lest we forget, of the awful cost of the Second World War. It is dedicated to the:

> ' . . . Memory of those who gave their lives
> Rest Eternal grant unto them O Lord and let
> Light perpetual shine upon them.'

TO COMMEMORATE THE USE OF
THIS CHURCH BY MEMBERS OF THE
FOLLOWING SQUADRONS OF THE
ROYAL AIR FORCE STATIONED AT
THE AERODROME HERE DURING
THE 1939 - 1945 WAR

No 218 GOLD COAST SQUADRON JULY
1942 MARH 44 STIRLING AIRCRAFT
No 623   SQUADRON AUGUST 1943
DEC.1943        STIRLING AIRCRAFT
No 214 SQUADRON DECEMBER 1943
JAN. 1944        STIRLING AIRCRAFT
No 635 SQUADRON MARCH 1944
MAY 1945 LANCASTER AIRCRAFT
No 608 SQUADRON AUGUST 1944
MAY 1945   MOSQUITO AIRCRAFT

And in Memory of those who
gave their lives Rest Eternal
grant unto them O Lord and let
Light Perpetual shine upon them

*Nearly one thousand airmen who flew from Downham Market gave their lives. A memorial to them can be found in St Mary's church, Bexwell*

# The Squadrons

## 214 (FEDERATED MALAY STATES) SQUADRON

Motto: *Ultor in umbris (Avenging in the shadows).*
At RAF Downham Market: December 1943 and January 1944.
Code letters: BU.
Commanding Officer: W/Cdr D. J. McGlinn, July 1943 – August 1944.

The squadron was originally formed in 1917 as 7A Squadron but was renumbered 214 Squadron on the establishment of the Royal Air Force in 1918. For most of the Second World War the squadron served in 3 Group. In September 1941 the squadron was adopted by the British Malayan Federation and had the words 'Federated Malay States' incorporated in its title. During the early part of 1942 it re-equipped with Short Stirling I's and then, on 11 December 1943, the squadron transferred from RAF Chedburgh, Suffolk, to join 218 Squadron at Downham Market. Its stay at Downham lasted just over a month. During its sojourn at Downham 214 Squadron made 36 operational sorties, including 25 to flying bomb sites and 11 mine-laying sorties. No aircraft were lost during this period. Between 17 and 20 January 1944 the squadron transferred again to RAF Sculthorpe.

*Badge of 214 (Federated Malay States) Squadron.*

*Stirling I as used by 214 Squadron.* Imperial War Museum MH5513

# 218 (GOLD COAST) SQUADRON

Motto: *In Time*.
At RAF Downham Market: July 1942 to March 1944.
Code letters: HA.
Commanding Officers; W/Cdr Walker, July – October 1942.
W/Cdr O.A. Morris, October 1942 – March 1943.
W/Cdr D.T. Saville, DSO, DFC, March – July 1943.
W/Cdr W.G. Oldbury, DFC, August 1943 – March 1944.

218 Squadron was originally formed in 1918 but disbanded the following year. It was re-formed in 1936 and became one of the very few bomber squadrons to serve continuously throughout the Second World War. In November 1940 the squadron converted from Bristol Blenheims to Vickers Wellingtons. At the same time it was transferred to 3 Group and moved to Marham. In 1941 the squadron was adopted by His Excellency the Governor of the Gold Coast and the peoples of the Gold Coast territories. On 7 July 1942 the squadron formally moved to Downham Market, which then became its home for the next twenty months.

The squadron had already begun converting to Short Stirling I's as early as February 1942 and a year later these were gradually replaced by the more powerful Short Stirling III. The Stirling was the first four-engined heavy bomber to be used by the Royal Air Force and with its 87 ft 3 in (26.59m) long fuselage was the largest aircraft to use Downham Market aerodrome regularly. During the second half of 1942 the squadron took part in many attacks on German

*Badge of 218 (Gold Coast) Squadron.*
Imperial War Museum CH15250

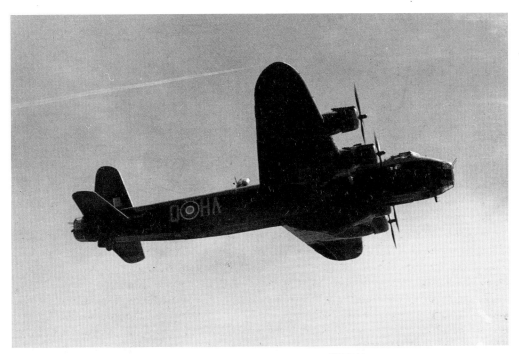

*Stirling I as used initially by 218 Squadron.* Imperial War Museum CH6310

targets as well as incursions into Italy and numerous mine-laying sorties. The missing rate for this period remained high at an average rate of 5.9 per cent, or almost one aircraft in every sixteen sorties.

Flight Sergeant A.L. Aaron was posthumously awarded the Victoria Cross for outstanding bravery during a raid on Turin on 12 August 1943. During the early part of 1943 attacks were made on submarine bases at Lorient and St Nazaire in France. Meanwhile the attacks on Germany were continued relentlessly until November when the squadron bombed Berlin for the last time. Thereafter, apart from attacks on flying-bomb sites in northern France in January and February 1944, the squadron was mostly engaged in mine-laying in the Bay of Biscay and the Baltic and the North Seas. 218 Squadron left Downham Market and moved to Woolfox Lodge on 7 March 1944.

218 Squadron flew 1,787 operational sorties (including 438 mine-laying sorties) while stationed at Downham Market. Seventy-seven aircraft failed to return from operations and twenty aircraft crashed in Britain. The inland targets most frequently attacked were: The Ruhr (196 sorties), Hamburg (121), Turin (65), Düsseldorf (64), Mannheim (62), Berlin (58), Cologne (54), Flying-bomb sites (47), Nuremberg (46), Frankfurt (46) and Stuttgart (34). Two of the squadron's aircraft flew considerably more operational sorties than the average. Stirling N3721 (variously coded C, J, P and S) flew a total of 61 sorties, the second highest for any Stirling, between March 1942 and July 1943. Stirling BK687 (code R) flew 54 sorties before failing to return.

# 571 SQUADRON

(No badge authorized)
At RAF Downham Market: April 1944.
Code letters: 8K.

Although the squadron was formed at Downham Market on 7 April 1944 as part of 8 (Pathfinder) Group's Light Night Striking Force no operations were ever carried out from the airfield. Plans were changed overnight and almost immediately after formation a detachment was sent to RAF Graveley where the squadron's first aircraft (de Haviland Mosquito XVI's) began operations. The rest of the squadron moved to Oakington between 22 and 24 April.

# 608 (NORTH RIDING) SQUADRON

Motto: *Omnibus ungulis (With all talons)*.
At RAF Downham Market: August 1944 to August 1945.
Code letters: 6T.
Commanding Officers: W/Cdr W.W.G. Scott, August – November 1944.
W/Cdr R.C. Alabaster, DSO, DFC, November 1944 – March 1945.
W/Cdr K. Gray, April – August 1945.

608 Squadron was originally formed in 1930 as an Auxiliary Air Force light-bomber squadron. Later it converted to general reconnaissance duties before being disbanded on 31 July 1944. The following day, on 1 August, 608 Squadron was re-formed at Downham Market as part of

*Mosquito BXVI as used by 571 Squadron.* Military Aircraft Photographs

8 (Pathfinder) Group's Light Night Striking Force operating de Haviland Mosquitos. Although largely constructed of wood the Mosquito was the most versatile and successful aircraft of the Second World War, its lightness and speed allowing it to be used in a variety of roles. At Downham it was used as a fast light bomber.

The squadron was initially equipped with Mosquito XX's. From October 1944 a few Mosquito 25's were added to the squadron and in March 1945 the squadron began converting to Mosquito XVI's. By the middle of April 1945 the squadron strength stood at sixteen Mosquito XVI's and ten Mosquito XX's and 25's. The first operation of the re-formed squadron was on 5/6 August 1944 when a single Mosquito bombed Wanne Eickel. Thereafter attacks on exclusively German targets continued unabated, rising to a crescendo in March 1945 when 276 sorties were carried out in that month alone. The final operation took place on 2 May 1945 when sixteen Mosquitos bombed Kiel in the RAF's last raid of the war. The squadron was disbanded on 24 August 1945 and its aircraft were moved to RAF Upper Heyford four days later.

608 squadron flew 1,685 sorties from Downham Market for the loss of only eleven aircraft. In addition seven aircraft crashed in Britain. The targets most frequently attacked were: Berlin (726 sorties), Hannover (135), The Ruhr (102), Hamburg (81), Nuremberg (57), Cologne (56), Brunswick (36), Kassel (36), Erfurt (35), Mannheim (35), Stuttgart (35), Frankfurt (34), Kiel (32), Karlsruhe (31) and Wiesbaden (31).

*Badge of 608 (North Riding) Squadron.*
Imperial War Museum CH16600

*Aircrews of 608 Squadron, September 1944.* C.R. Jacobs

*F/Lt George A. Nunn DFC.*

*Crew of Stirling B-Berty, 623 Squadron, with their aircraft in the background.*

# 623 SQUADRON

(No badge authorized)
At RAF Downham Market: August to December 1943.
Code letters: IC.
Commanding Officer: W/Cdr E.J. Little, DFC, August 1943.
W/Cdr G.T. Wynne-Powell, September – November 1943.
W/Cdr F.M. Milligan, AFC, December 1943.

The squadron was formed at Downham Market on 10 August 1943 from one flight of 218 Squadron. It was intended to become a two-flight squadron with sixteen operational aircraft and four aircraft in reserve, but a change in plans led to 623 Squadron's disbandment and replacement by 214 Squadron in early December. During its short life the squadron operated Short Stirling bombers. The squadron flew 137 operational sorties of which 94 were bombing and 43 were mine-laying. Ten aircraft failed to return from operations and one aircraft crashed on the airfield. The main targets attacked were Berlin and Mannheim (each 15 sorties).

*Aircrews of 623 Squadron, October 1943.* Len Warner

# 635 SQUADRON

Motto: *Nos ducimus ceteri secunter (We lead, others follow).*
At RAF Downham Market: March 1944 to September 1945.
Code letters: F2.
Commanding Officers: W/Cdr A.G.S. Cousens, March – April 1944.
W/Cdr W.T. Brooks, April – June 1944.
W/Cdr S. Baker, DSO, DFC, July 1944 – March 1945.
W/Cdr J. Fordham, March – September 1945.

The squadron was formed in 8 (Pathfinder) Group, at Downham Market on 20 March 1944. On formation it comprised sixteen Avro Lancasters from the B Flight of 35 Squadron and the C Flight of 97 Squadron. The Lancaster was undoubtedly the finest British heavy bomber of the Second World War. It could carry up to 14,000 lb (6,350 kg) of bombs and had a top speed of 287 mph (462 km/h).

The first raid took place two days after the squadron's establishment when ten aircraft (out of fourteen scheduled to take part) bombed Frankfurt. After a few more raids on German targets the squadron was switched to attacking targets in northern France in preparation for the forthcoming Normandy invasion. The squadron continued to attack targets in France, interspersed with a limited number of German targets, until the end of September. During this

*Badge of 635 Squadron.* Imperial War Museum CH16672

*Wg/Cdr S. 'Tubby' Baker DSO & Bar, DFC & Bar, OC 635 Squadron, July 1944–March 1945.* Wg/Cdr S. Baker.

*Lancaster VI as used by 635 Squadron.* via B. Robertson

*Aircrews of 635 Squadron, May 1945.* W.A. Rumble, via A.C. Hartley

phase Squadron Leader I.W. Bazalgette was posthumously awarded the Victoria Cross for outstanding bravery during a daylight raid on a flying-bomb site in northern France on 4 August.

The squadron was selected to carry out operational trials with the new Lancaster Mark VI between July and November. These aircraft had their nose and dorsal turrets removed to increase performance and were equipped with improved H2S radar bombing aids. On 10 August three of the Lancaster VI's were used to drop Bomber Command's first 10,000 lb bombs in a raid on Bremen.

Apart from one raid to Bergen, Norway, on 4 October and three aids to targets in Holland all of the squadron's remaining raids were on German targets. The final raids were to Hitler's mountain retreat at Berchtesgaden and to Wangerooge (both on 25 April 1945). In May 1945 the squadron took part in dropping food supplies to the beleaguered Dutch in western Holland and in carrying ex-prisoners-of-war back to Britain from Belgium. The squadron was disbanded on 1 September 1945.

635 Squadron flew 2,099 operational sorties from Downham Market. Thirty-four aircraft failed to return from operations and a further seven aircraft were destroyed in crashes in Britain. The targets most frequently attacked were: The Ruhr (352 sorties), Kiel (78), Hamburg (73), Nuremberg (47), Düsseldorf (43), Stuttgart (43), Cologne (42), Calais (41), Chemnitz (32), Bremen (31), Russelheim (31) and Caen (30). Lancaster ND709 (code J) had the longest service and flew more than a hundred sorties. It began life with 35 Squadron but was handed over to 635 Squadron in April 1944. The plane's one-hundredth sortie was completed on 14 February 1945 with a raid on Chemnitz.

## SORTIES DISPATCHED AND AIRCRAFT LOST FROM RAF DOWNHAM MARKET

| Year | No. of Sorties | No. of Aircraft Lost | Percentage of Aircraft Lost | Squadron Nos. Involved |
|------|------|------|------|------|
| 1942 | 517 | 40 | 7.7 | 218 |
| 1943 | 1268 | 65 | 5.1 | 214, 218, 623 |
| 1944 | 2500 | 40 | 1.6 | 214, 218, 608, 635 |
| 1945 | 1480 | 15 | 1.0 | 608, 635 |

NOTE: 'Number of Aircraft Lost' includes all aircraft which failed to return *and* aircraft which crashed in Britain while taking part in offensive operations. The figures do not include aircraft which crashed on test or training flights.

# Notes

1 Both quotations are taken from *Airmail*, Spring 1985, p. 13
2 In December 1944 the station's population of 2,045 was made up of:
RAF Officers – 185; RAF SNCOs – 262; RAF Other Ranks – 1,272
WAAF Officers – 8; WAAF SNCOs – 8; WAAF Other Ranks – 310
3 Public Record Office, AIR 27-1350
4 *Lynn News and Advertiser*, 8 June 1945
5 David J. Smith: *Britain's Military Airfields 1939–45*, p. 141
6 Quoted from Paul W. Dascombe: *We Lead, Others Follow*, p. 30
7 In 1943 pay in different RAF trade groups varied from two shillings and six-pence (12½p) to seventeen shillings (85p) per day
8 The verses at the beginning of Chapters 4–7 are from 'We, The Bombers', by P. Heath
9 Quoted from 'Archie' Hall (ed.): *We, Also, Were There*, p. 47
10 Ibid., pp. 108–9
11 Quoted from Martin Middlebrook: *The Battle of Hamburg – The Firestorm Raid* (1980), p. 117
12 Quoted from: *Aeroplane Monthly*, November 1977, p. 569
13 Public Record Office, AIR 27-1350
14 Information from Bob Fuller, Downham Market
15 Quoted from Laddie Lucas (ed.): *Out of the Blue*, p. 285
16 Quoted from Jonathan Falconer: *Stirling at War*, p. 60
17 218 Squadron Operations Record Book (Public Record Office, AIR 27-1351)
18 Combat Report (Public Record Office, AIR 50-234)
19 Quoted from Martin Middlebrook: *The Nuremberg Raid, 30–31 March 1944* (revised edn 1980), pp. 142–3
20 Combat report (Public Record Office, AIR 50-288)
21 Quoted from: *A Short History of R.A.F. Station Downham Market*, p. 2. This was a ten-page typescript written in 1945. The anonymous author was probably serving with 635 Squadron
22 Ibid., p. 3
23 Ibid., p. 4
24 Quoted from unpublished diary notes of operations 1944/45
25 Quoted from Paul W. Dascombe: *We Lead, Others Follow*, p. 17
26 Quoted from Alexander McKee: *The Mosquito Log*, p. 140
27 Ibid., pp. 143–5
28 Ibid, p. 146
29 Peenemünde rocket research site, 17 August 1943
30 Quoted from Paul W. Dascombe: *We Lead, Others Follow*, p. 30
31 Quoted from Murray Peden: *A Thousand Shall Fall*, pp. 319–20
32 Information by P/O E. Pierce, 218 and 623 Squadrons, via John Reid
33 Quoted from *Lynn News and Advertiser*, 17 April 1945
34 Quoted from Alex Thorne: *Lancaster at War 4: Pathfinder Squadron*, p. 82
35 According to figures quoted in *The Bomber Command War Diaries* (p. 708), by M. Middlebrook and G. Everitt, 82.7 per cent of all missing bomber aircrew were killed. Estimated casualty figures for Downham Market are based on this percentage
36 Quoted from Alfred Price: *The fate of R.A.F. Stirling BK712*, pp. 27–8. Price refers to W. Skillinglaw, but the name given by the Commonwealth War Graves Commission is William Golder Shillinglaw
37 Quoted from: *A Short History of R.A.F. Station Downham Market*, p. 1
38 Ibid., p. 2
39 Quoted from: *Eastern Daily Press*, 18 August 1983
40 Quoted from: *The London Gazette*, 5 November 1943
41 Ibid., 17 August 1945
42 Quoted from Paul W. Dascombe: *We Lead, Others Follow*, p. 29
43 Quoted from Bill Jackson: *Three Stripes and Four Brownings*, pp. 261–2

44   Dulag Luft was the main interrogation centre and transit camp for RAF prisoners-of-war
45   This account of the forced march is based on Aidan Crawley: *Escape from Germany*, chapters 17, 32 and 38
46   Quoted from: M.I.9 de-briefing statement, 7 September 1944 (Public Record Office, WO-208)
47   Ibid., 21 January 1944 (Public Record Office, WO-208)
48   Quoted from Bill Jackson: *Three Stripes and Four Brownings*, p. 110
49   Quoted from: I.S.9 de-briefing statement, 9 August 1944 (Public Record Office, WO-208)
50   Ibid., 9 August 1945
51   Quoted from: I.S.9 de-briefing statement, 19 November 1945 (Public Record Office, WO-208)
52   Quoted from: M.I.9 de-briefing statement, 25 June 1945 (Public Record Office, WO-208)
53   Quoted from Paul W. Dascombe: *We Lead, Others Follow*, p. 9
54   Quoted from Alex Thorne: *Lancaster at War 4: Pathfinder Squadron*, pp. 125–6
55   Quoted from: *Lynn News and Advertiser*, 4 September 1945
56   Ibid., 18 September 1945

# Bibliography

Anonymous, 'Hangars on the Bomber Bases', in *Airfield Review*, vol. 10, No. 4, Airfield Research Group, December 1989

Anonymous, *A Short History of R.A.F. Station Downham Market* (A ten page typescript, written in 1945)

Barker, Ralph, *The Thousand Plan*, Chatto & Windus, 1965

Bowyer, Chaz, *Bomber Barons*, William Kimber, 1983

Bowyer, Michael, J. F., *Action Stations 1; East Anglia*, Patrick Stephens Ltd, 1979

——, *The Stirling Bomber*, Faber & Faber, 1980

——, *Air Raid! The Enemy Air Offensive Against East Anglia, 1939–1945*, Patrick Stephens Ltd, 1986

Crawley, Aidan, *Escape from Germany*, Dorset Press (New York), 1985

Falconer, Jonathan, *Stirling at War*, Ian Allan Ltd, 1991

Gomersall, Bryce, *The Stirling File*, Air Britain and Aviation Archaeologist, 1979

Goulding, James, and Moyes, Philip, *R.A.F. Bomber Command and its Aircraft 1941–1945*, Ian Allan Ltd, 1978

Hall, 'Archie', *We, Also, Were There*, Merlin Books, 1985

Hastings, Max, *Bomber Command*, Michael Joseph, 1979

Jackson, Bill, *Three Stripes and Four Brownings*, Turner-Warwick Publications Inc, Canada, 1990

Kinsey, Gordon, *Aviation: Flight over the Eastern Counties since 1937*, Terence Dalton, 1977

Longmate, Norman, *The Bombers*, Hutchinson, 1983

Lucas, Laddie, *Out of the Blue*, Hutchinson, 1985

McKee, Alexander, *The Mosquito Log*, Souvenier Press, 1988

Middlebrook, Martin, *The Battle of Hamburg*, Allen Lane, 1984

——, *The Nuremberg Raid*, Allen Lane, 1973, 1980

——, and Everitt, Chris, *The Bomber Command War Diaries*, Viking, 1985

Mondey, David, *British Aircraft of World War II*, Hamlyn/Aerospace, 1982

Moyes, Philip, J. R., *Bomber Squadrons of the R.A.F. and Their Aircraft*, Macdonald, 1964

Musgrave, Gordon, *Pathfinder Force*, Macdonald & Jane's, 1976

Peden, Murray, *A Thousand Shall Fall*, Canada's Wings, 1979, Imperial War Museum, 1981

Richards, Denis, and Saunders, Hilary St George, *Royal Air Force 1939–45*, HMSO, 1953

Robertson, Bruce, *Lancaster: The Story of a Famous Bomber*, Harleyford, 1964

Sharp, C. Martin, and Bowyer, Michael J. F., *Mosquito*, Faber & Faber, 1967, 1971

Smith, David J., *De Haviland Mosquito Crash Log*, Midland Counties, 1980

——, *Britain's Military Airfields 1939–45*, Patrick Stephens Ltd, 1989

Taylor, Geoff, *The Nuremberg Massacre*, Hutchinson of Australia, 1979

Thompson, Walter, *Lancaster to Berlin*, Goodall, 1985

Thorne, Alex, *Lancaster at War 4: Pathfinder Squadron*, Ian Allan Ltd, 1990

# Index of Operations

Note: While the following list of operations referred to in the text covers only a small proportion of those actually carried out it does give a reasonably fair representation of targets attacked at each period during the life of the airfield.

| Date | Squadron(s) | Target | Page |
|---|---|---|---|
| 30 May 1942 | 115 & 218 | Cologne | 8 |
| 01 June 1942 | 115 & 218 | Essen | 9 |
| 12 July 1942 | 218 | Frisian Islands – mining | 11 |
| 13 July 1942 | 218 | Duisburg | 11 |
| 28 July 1942 | 218 | Hamburg | 11 |
| 20 Aug 1942 | 218 | Kiel Bay – mining | 55 |
| 24 Aug 1942 | 218 | Frankfurt | 87 |
| 28 Aug 1942 | 218 | Saarbrucken | 44 |
| 17 Oct 1942 | 218 | Bornholm & Rugen – mining | 56 |
| 28 Nov 1942 | 218 | Turin | 55 |
| 17 Dec 1942 | 218 | Fallersleben | 50 |
| | | | |
| 27 Jan 1943 | 218 | Baltic mining | 96 |
| 14 Apr 1943 | 218 | Stuttgart | 50 |
| 14 May 1943 | 218 | Bochum | 50, 82 |
| 21 June 1943 | 218 | Krefeld | 88 |
| 22 June 1943 | 218 | Mulheim | 78 |
| 24 July 1943 | 218 | Hamburg | 52, 88 |
| 27 July 1943 | 218 | Hamburg | 54 |
| 29 July 1943 | 218 | Hamburg | 54 |
| 02 Aug 1943 | 218 | Hamburg | 54–5 |
| 12 Aug 1943 | 218 | Turin | 89, 116 |
| 16 Aug 1943 | 218 | Turin | 98–9 |
| 17 Aug 1943 | 218 | Peenemünde | 75 |
| 27 Aug 1943 | 623 | Nuremberg | 88 |
| 30 Aug 1943 | 218 | Mönchengladbach | 94, 100 |
| 02 Sep 1943 | 218 | Frisian Islands – mining | 58 |
| 03 Sep 1943 | 218 | La Rochelle – mining | 58 |
| 05 Sep 1943 | 218 | Mannheim | 58 |
| 09 Sep 1943 | 218 | Boulogne | 58 |
| 15 Sep 1943 | 218 | Montluçon | 58 |
| 16 Sep 1943 | 218 | Modane | 58 |
| 03 Oct 1943 | 218 | North Sea – mining | 58 |
| 04 Oct 1943 | 218 | Frankfurt | 58 |
| 25 Oct 1943 | 218 | Baltic Sea – mining | 58 |
| 04 Nov 1943 | 218 | Kattegat – mining | 55 |
| 18 Nov 1943 | 218 | Mannheim | 58, 94 |
| 19 Nov 1943 | 218 | Leverkusen | 58 |
| 22 Nov 1943 | 218 | Berlin | 58 |
| 31 Dec 1943 | 214 & 218 | Dutch coast – mining | 56 |
| | | | |
| 05 Jan 1944 | 218 | Le Touquet & Abbeville | 58 |
| 06 Jan 1944 | 218 | San Sebastian – mining | 59 |
| 14 Jan 1944 | 218 | Cherbourg | 59 |

| Date | Squadron(s) | Target | Page |
|------|-------------|--------|------|
| 29 Jan 1944 | 218 | Kiel Harbour | 59 |
| 12 Feb 1944 | 218 | Frisian Islands – mining | 59 |
| 15 Feb 1944 | 218 | Kiel Harbour – mining | 59 |
| 17 Feb 1944 | 218 | North Sea – mining | 59 |
| 19 Feb 1944 | 218 | Kiel Harbour – mining | 59 |
| 21 Feb 1944 | 218 | Frisian Islands – mining | 59 |
| 22 Feb 1944 | 218 | Kiel Harbour – mining | 59 |
| 30 Mar 1944 | 635 | Nuremberg | 62, 96 |
| 18 Apr 1944 | 635 | Rouen | 89 |
| 22 Apr 1944 | 635 | Laon | 89, 98 |
| 27 Apr 1944 | 635 | Friedrichshafen | 63 |
| 20 May 1944 | 635 | Duisberg | 100 |
| 05 June 1944 | 635 | Normandy Coast | 63 |
| 11 June 1944 | 635 | Nantes | 63, 101 |
| 15 June 1944 | 635 | Lens | 102 |
| 22 June 1944 | 635 | Siracourt Rocket Site | 64 |
| 04 Aug 1944 | 635 | Trossy-St-Maxim V1 Site | 91 |
| 05 Aug 1944 | 608 | Wanne Eickel | 118 |
| 10 Aug 1944 | 635 | Bremen | 122 |
| 26 Aug 1944 | 635 | Kiel | 97 |
| 29 Aug 1944 | 635 | Stettin | 65 |
| 04 Oct 1944 | 635 | Bergen | 40, 122 |
| 30 Oct 1944 | 635 | Cologne | 106 |
| 30 Nov 1944 | 635 | Duisberg | 106 |
| 11 Dec 1944 | 608 | Duisberg | 73 |
| 24 Dec 1944 | 635 | Düsseldorf Airfield | 81 |
| 14 Feb 1945 | 608 & 635 | Chemnitz, Mainz & Berlin | 72, 123 |
| 17 Feb 1945 | 635 | Wessel | 80 |
| 05 Mar 1945 | 608 | Berlin | 68 |
| 13 Mar 1945 | 635 | Wuppertal | 66, 106 |
| 25 Mar 1945 | 635 | Osnabrück | 46 |
| 09 Apr 1945 | 635 | Kiel | 106 |
| 10 Apr 1945 | 635 | Leipzig | 106 |
| 11 Apr 1945 | 635 | Nuremberg | 106 |
| 13 Apr 1945 | 608 | Hamburg | 106 |
| 20 Apr 1945 | 608 | Berlin | 106 |
| 21 Apr 1945 | 608 | Kiel | 106 |
| 22 Apr 1945 | 635 | Bremen | 106 |
| 25 Apr 1945 | 608 | Munich | 106 |
| 25 Apr 1945 | 635 | Berchtesgaden & Wangerooge | 107, 125 |
| 26 Apr 1945 | 608 | Eggebek Airfield | 108 |
| 02 May 1945 | 608 | Kiel | 108, 122 |

# Index of People and Places

Note: Page numbers in italics denote illustrations.